THE CONSOLIDATED GOSPEL OF JESUS CHRIST, THE SON OF GOD

JOHN MANOHAR RAJAN

Copyright © John Manohar Rajan
All Rights Reserved.

I dedicate this work to Lord my Savior Jesus Christ. Because

"I was nothing until He found me. . .

He had given me life

Contents

Preface   *ix*

Consolidation - Why?   *xi*

Introduction   *xvii*

THE BIRTH OF CHRIST AND HIS CHILDHOOD

1. Birth Of John The Baptist   3

2. Birth Of Christ   8

3. Life Of Christ Till He Was Thirty Years Old   15

MINISTRY OF JESUS CHRIST

4. John The Baptist   23

5. The Beginning Of Christ's Ministry   29

6. Ministry's Base Shifted To Galilee   36

7. Christ In Jerusalem   41

8. Difference Of Opinion With The Religious Leaders In Galilee   49

9. Sermon On The Mount   53

10. Ministry With The Apostles   64

11. A Sermon Of Parables   69

12. The Wind, The Waves And The Legion   74

13. Powerful Ministry Of Jesus Christ And The Doubts Of John The Baptist   77

14. The Ministerial Journey Continues Via Nazareth   82

15. The Harvest Is Plentiful But The Workers Are Few   84

16. The Execution Of John The Baptist   88

THE FINAL YEAR OF CHRIST'S MINISTRY

17. The First Part Of The Final Year   97

18. The Transfiguration   104

19. The Feast Of Tabernacles In Jerusalem   111

20. Journey From Galilee To Jerusalem For The Last Time   124

21. To Jerusalem Through Jericho   130

Contents

THE FINAL WEEK OF JESUS CHRIST

22. Six Days Before The Passover (Saturday - The Sabbath Day)   137

23. The Next Day (Sunday)   140

24. The Cleansing Of Temple (Monday)   142

25. Last Sermon Of Jesus In The Temple (Tuesday)   144

26. Mary Pays Her (last) Respect (Wednesday)   162

27. The Last Passover Of Jesus Christ (Thursday)   165

28. The Betrayal And Arrest At The Garden Of Gethsemane (Thursday Night)   175

29. The Jewish (trial!) Plot To Kill (Friday)   178

30. The Roman Trial   182

31. The Suffering And Death   186

32. The Tomb Sealed (Saturday The Sabbath)   191

HE HAS RISEN JUST AS HE SAID

33. The First Day Of The Week (sunday)   195

34. Resurrected Jesus - Back In Galilee   202

35. Taken Up Into Heaven - At The Mount Of Olives   205

36. The Institution Of The Church   207

I would like to acknowledge the prayers and words of encouragements from numerous well wishers without which it would not have been possible for me to accomplish a task of this magnitude. May God bless them.

PREFACE

We come to know about the life, ministry and teachings of Jesus Christ the Son of God through the Gospels according to Matthew, Mark, Luke and John in the Holy Bible. The narration of events in these Gospels is very simple. But they are not as simple as they seem to be, when it comes to understanding them.

When a copy of the New Testament was gifted to a non - Christian person, he started to read it from the begining in all sincerity. As we know the first chapter of Matthew with which the New Testament begins, starts with the genealogy of Jesus Christ. After reading a verses of "So and so begat so and so....", the non - Christian friend was put off. He took a pen and wrote at the end of the chapternames of his father and himself saying "So and so begat so and so" and closed the book for good!

The Gospel according to John is the most commanly Gospel presented to a new believer. Unfortunately quite a few of them donot get to read the whole Gospel just because they donot understand the first page of it.

Apart from the differences between the gospel narrations- portrayed as contradictions by biblical critics, no single Gospel gives us the full story that is right from the birth of John the Baptist befor the birth of Christ ot the institution of the church- after the ascension of Christ. To get to know the full story, one has to go back and forth the four Gospels.

Considering these facts I the need to present the Gospel story in a easy to understand format, where the differences between the gospel narrations are reconciled and the events are given in chronological order.

Since the Gospel writters have no reason to lie, I presumed that every satement they made in their Gospel accounts is true. Then I took the simple logics we use in our day- to- day life and applied them to resolve the differences in the Gospel accounts. As I ventured into this attempt, I was amazed to see the very part of the Gospel accounts fall into its respective place anf forming a clear anf full picture of the life, teacing and ministry of Jesus Christ.

What's more, apostle John provides the perfect introduction Mark gives the note of conclution!

Consolidation - Why?

The apparent differences in the accounts given by the four Gospel writers while narrating the events in the life of Lord Jesus Christ could confuse a reader – especially one who takes time to go through them in detail, comparing each account with the others.

Following a bank robbery, three eyewitnesses were brought to the investigating officer. The officer was at first relived that his job would be made easier by the corroborative evidence given by more than one eyewitness. But soon his joy turned into disbelief as, when to his dismay, he saw that there were numerous differences and apparent contradictions in the details given by those three witnesses for the one and the same incident.

He tabulated the details obtained from the three witnesses as follows:

	Witness 1	Witness 2	Witness 3
1	There were five robbers.	There were three robbers.	There were five robbers.
2	They scared the public as they entered the bank by detonating a grenade.	We heard a big blast as they made their way inside.	They barged into the bank suddenly, threatened us with dire consequences, and began to rob the bank.
3	They first entered the manager's office, attacked him, and took him hostage.	As soon as they entered, they attacked the manager and cashier.	At the same time, they attacked and injured the bank staff.
4	After robbing the bank, when leaving, they dragged the manager along with them.	After securing the booty, they fired a few shots into the floor to terrorize the people around, then left in great haste.	All five of them escaped in three getaway vehicles and did not take the manager with them.

The officer was puzzled as to what to conclude.

- Were there three robbers, or five?
- Which of the bank staff were attacked?
- The Manager alone?
- Or was it the Manager and Cashier, or all of the bank staff?
- Was the manager dragged along and taken away by the robbers or not?

Unable to make out anything from these details, he decided to approach his superior for guidance. When his experienced superior went through these accounts, he came up with two important conclusions. All three statements were <u>true,</u> and that on <u>consolidating these three accounts, more truth </u>is revealed than by any one single account alone. These conclusions of his superior, using the very same details that had puzzled him, surprised the investigating officer.

The senior officer, in order to lend a helping hand to his junior, then consolidated the eyewitness accounts for him. The details obtained by this consolidation are as follows:

1. The total number of robbers was five (it is possible that two of them stood guard out side while only three entered the bank to execute their plan. Probably witness 2 did not notice the two who were standing guard.)
2. As they entered the bank, they exploded a grenade and scared the public.
3. Though they attacked both the manager and cashier of the bank, the former was attacked first. The robbers first entered the manager's office, attacked him, and then took him hostage. They then attacked the cashier also before looting the place.
4. After completing the robbery, the robbers dragged the manager along with, them while at the same time, fired a few shots on the floor to terrorize the people. As soon as they exited the bank, they let the manager go and escaped with the loot in three escape vehicles.

Likewise, with all four Gospel accounts being **TRUE**, when a similar effort is made to consolidate them, **MORE REVELATION OF TRUTH is** obtained. Whats more, difficult to explain portions find easy and logical solutions in the consolidated form.

Following are a few examples of such portions that make little sense before consolidation:

(Jn. 1:31) The purpose of John's ministry was to identify Christ to the Israelites (Jn. 1:31, 33) and the sign to identify Christ is that the Spirit comes down and remains.

(Mt. 3:16) The Holy Spirit came down <u>only after Jesus was baptized</u>, therefore, only then John could have known Jesus to be the Christ.

(Mt. 3:14) If that was so, then how did John recognize Jesus as the Christ and try to deter Him <u>before the baptism itself</u>?

(Mt. 28:5-9) Jesus met the women, including Mary Magdalene, returning from the tomb after hearing from the angel.

(Lk. 24:9-11) They told all these things to the eleven apostles. That being the case, how are we to explain the following?

(Mk. 16:9) Jesus appeared first to Mary Magdalene. (Jn. 20:2-8) Peter and John ran to the tomb to see.

The solution to questions like these is obtained when we consolidate the four gospels, just as the senior officer had done with the robbery eyewitness accounts.

What is interesting is that from the consolidated gospel, we not only get the needed solutions, but also more truth than which is otherwise known. As a result, this very exercise was a rewarding experience.

[Note:

I have used The New International Version in this consolidation. The four Gospels, and the first two chapters of the Acts of Apostles, all put together contain 3,852 verses. Of these, the consolidated Gospel is made from 3,846. Only six verses i.e., Lk. 1:1-4 and Acts 1:1,2 have been left out.. All the rest have been accounted for.]

In this effort to consolidate the four Gospel accounts, I have adhered to a few general rules. They are as follows:

RULE – I: In case of numerical difference between two Gospel accounts, the higher number is taken as the more precise one.

Example: Mt. 8:28 / Mk. 5:2 – In these portions, Mathew talks about two people while Mark describes only one person. Therefore to resolve this issue by Rule – I, we understand that there were actually two people, and Mathew accounts for both of them, while Mark describes only one of them.

RULE – II: Of the four Gospel authors, Mark gives the most importance to the **chronological sequence** of eventsin his presentation. Next to him, more than either Luke or John, Mathew gives the next most importance to it. Therefore, in my effort to consolidate the Gospels for the chronological sequence, I have relied primarily on Mark and Mathew.

RULE – III: There are incidents given in the Gospels that have many similarities between them. To determine if these incidents are actually **two different incidents** or repetition in narration of **one and the same**, the two conditions given below are used for reference.

If the given incident satisfies either condition, then we can be sure that it is a case of two different incidents. On the other hand, if it does not satisfy even one of the below given conditions, then it is probably a case of repetition in narration.

Condition – I:

The incidents with many similarities must be given twice in a same Gospel.

Example: Mt. 10:1-15 / Lk. 10:1-12

This example satisfies the first condition because in the same Gospel of Luke, we have another incident given, in another section/chapter, which is similar to the above quoted incident (Lk. 9:1-5).

The two incidents quoted in Lk. 9 & Lk. 10 have many similarities between them. But since it is repeated twice in the book of Luke itself, we can safely conclude that Jesus sent out His people on two separate occasions for ministry (12 Apostles /70 Followers), giving similar instructions each time.

Condition – II:

If the incidents with many similarities are not given twice in the same Gospel, then the circumstances, the purpose and other things about them should vary considerably, enabling us to conclude that these two are surely two different incidents and not just a mere repetition in narration.

Example: (Mt. 26:6-13 / Mk. 14:3-9 / Jn. 12:1-8) and (Lk. 7:36-50).

In the above quoted portions, Mathew, Mark and John are referring to the same incidents. But Luke is narrating an entirely different incident.

Though this example does not satisfy Condition – I, as the incident is narrated only once in every Gospel, it satisfies Condition – II, as the differences between them, given below, are obvious.

		LUKE	OTHERS
1	Place of the incident	Galilee	Judea (Bethany)
2	The host	A Pharisee	Simon (who was a leper)
3	The woman who applied the perfume	A sinful woman	Mary who was delivered from seven evil spirits
4	The part of Jesus' body to which the perfume was applied	Feet	Head and Foot

Apart from the above-mentioned differences, if we listen to the comments from those around, and the reply Jesus gave to them, they were each totally different. So it is conclusively known that these are two completely different incidents.

Similarly, if any two incidents that look similar but do not satisfy even one of the above said conditions, we can safely conclude that they are a repetition in narration only.

Another example of this is found in Mt. 21:12-13/Mk. 11:15-17 and Jn. 2:13-17/ Lk. 19:45-46. John in his Gospel says that the cleansing of the temple was done in the first Passover of Christ's ministry. But the other three Gospel writers all state that it was done only in the fourth (last) Passover.

To answer the question about whether Jesus cleansed the temple twice (first and fourth Passover) or only once i.e., in the last Passover, we have to subject it to the two conditions of Rule – III.

Condition – I: This incident is not repeated twice but given only once in every Gospel. Therefore it fails this condition.

Condition – II: When the narration given by Mathew, Mark and Luke are compared with that given by John, there is not much difference between them to suggest that they are two different incidents. Therefore it fails this condition too.

Since it fails to satisfy even one of the condition of Rule – III we can assume that the cleansing of the temple was done only once.

RULE – IV: To decide the chronological sequence of different events, the particular event should have been stated either

- To follow the aforementioned event,

    (Or)

- That it precedes the following event in at least one of the four Gospels. Example: Lk. 13:31-35 "...today... tomorrow... reach my goal..." Mt. 23:37-39 "O Jerusalem! Jerusalem! !..."

Though the above-mentioned passage from Luke occurs in a different place in the Gospel of Luke, it is still placed in the third day of the final week of Christ's life by applying this Rule.

I now heartily welcome you to read and find out **comprehensively** what actually happened in the life of **Lord Jesus Christ**.

Introduction

(Jn. 1:1-18)

In the beginning was the Word, and the Word was with God, and the Word was God. He was with God in the beginning.

Through him all things were made; without him nothing was made that has been made. In him was life, and that life was the light of men. The light shines in the darkness, but the darkness has not overcome it.

There came a man who was sent from God; his name was John. He came as a witness to testify concerning that light, so that through him all men might believe. He himself was not the light; he came only as a witness to the light. The true light that gives light to every man was coming into the world.

He was in the world, and though the world was made through him, the world did not recognize him. He came to that which was his own, but his own did not receive him. Yet to all who received him, to those who believed in his name, he gave the right to become children of God – children born not of natural descent, nor of human decision or a husband's will, but born of God.

The Word became flesh and made his dwelling among us. We have seen his glory, the glory of the One and only, who came from the Father, full of grace and truth.

John testifies concerning him. He cries out, saying, "This was he of whom I said, 'He who comes after me has surpassed me because he was before me.'" From the fullness of his grace we have all received one blessing after another. For the law was given through Moses; grace and truth came through Jesus Christ. No one has ever seen God, but God the One and only, who is at the Father's side, has made him known.

(Mk. 1:1)

[*This is*] the beginning of the Gospel about Jesus Christ, the Son of God.

THE BIRTH OF CHRIST AND HIS CHILDHOOD

I
BIRTH OF JOHN THE BAPTIST

(Lk. 1:5-56)

In the time of Herod king of Judea there was a priest named Zechariah, who belonged to the priestly division of Abijah; his wife Elizabeth was also a descendant of Aaron. Both of them were upright in the sight of God, observing all the Lord's commandments and regulations blamelessly. But they had no children, because Elizabeth was barren; and they were both well along in years.

Once when Zechariah's division was on duty and he was serving as priest before God, he was chosen by lot, according to the custom of the priesthood, to go into the temple of the Lord and burn incense. And when the time for the burning of incense came, all the assembled worshipers were praying outside.

Then an angel of the Lord appeared to him, standing at the right side of the altar of incense. When Zechariah saw him, he was startled and was gripped with fear. But the angel said to him: "Do not be afraid, Zechariah; your prayer has been heard. Your wife Elizabeth will bear you a son, and you are to give him the name John. He will be a joy and delight to you, and many will rejoice because of his birth, for he will be great in the sight of the Lord. He is never to take wine or other fermented drink, and he will be filled with the Holy Spirit from his mother's womb. Many of the people of Israel will he bring back to the Lord their God. And he will go on before the Lord, in the spirit and power of Elijah, to turn the hearts of the fathers to their children and the disobedient to the wisdom of the righteous – to make ready a people prepared for the Lord."

Zechariah asked the angel, "How can I be sure of this? I am an old man, and my wife is well along in years."

The angel answered, "I am Gabriel. I stand in the presence of God, and I have been sent to speak to you and to tell you this good news. And now you will be silent and not able to speak until the day this happens, because you did not believe my words, which will come true at their proper time."

Meanwhile, the people were waiting for Zechariah and wondering why he stayed so long in the temple. When he came out, he could not speak to them. They realized he had seen a vision in the temple, for he kept making signs to them but remained unable to speak.

When his time of service was completed, he returned home. After this his wife Elizabeth became pregnant and for five months remained in seclusion. "The Lord has done this for me," she said. "In these days he has shown his favor and taken away my disgrace among the people." [*These happened in Judea.*]

In the sixth month, God sent the angel Gabriel [*This is the same Angel who appeared to Zechariah*]to Nazareth, a town in Galilee, to a virgin pledged to be married to a man named Joseph, a descendant of David. The virgin's name was Mary. The angel went to her and said, "Greetings, you who are highly favored! The Lord is with you."

Mary was greatly troubled at his words and wondered what kind of greeting this might be. But the angel said to her, "Do not be afraid, Mary, you have found favor with God. You will be with child and give birth to a son, and you are to give him the name Jesus. He will be great and will be called the Son of the Most High. The Lord God will give him the throne of his father David, and he will reign over the house of Jacob forever; his kingdom will never end."

"How will this be," Mary asked the angel, "since I am a virgin?" [*She is already pledged to Joseph, but they are yet to be married.*]

The angel answered, "The Holy Spirit will come upon you, and the power of the Most High will overshadow you. So the holy one to be born will be called the Son of God. Even Elizabeth your relative is going to have a child in her old age, and she who was said to be barren is in her sixth month. For nothing is impossible with God."

"I am the Lord's servant," Mary answered. "May it be to me as you have said." Then the angel left her.

At that time Mary got ready and hurried to a town in the hill country of Judea [*she must have left within a few days after being informed by the angel*], where she entered Zechariah's home and greeted Elizabeth.

When Elizabeth heard Mary's greeting, the baby leaped in her womb, and Elizabeth was filled with the Holy Spirit. In a loud voice she exclaimed: "Blessed are you among women, and blessed is the child you will bear! But why am I so favored, that the mother of my Lord should come to me? As soon as the sound of your greeting reached my ears, the baby in my womb leaped for joy. Blessed is she who has believed that what the Lord has said to her will be accomplished!"

And Mary said:

"My soul glorifies the Lord

and my spirit rejoices in God my Savior

for he has been mindful

of the humble state of his servant.

From now on all generations will call me blessed for the Mighty One has done great things for me –

holy is his name.

His mercy extends to those who fear him,

From generation to generation.

He has performed mighty deeds with his arm;

he has scattered those who are proud in their in most thoughts.

He has brought down rulers from their thrones

but has lifted up the humble.

He has filled the hungry with good things

but has sent the rich away empty.

He has helped his servant Israel,

remembering to be merciful

to Abraham and his descendants forever,

even as he said to our fathers." [*This is an indication of Mary's knowledge about Prophesies and Promises from the Lord.*]

Mary stayed with Elizabeth for about three months and then returned home. [*By this time Elizabeth should have been full-term pregnant.*]

(Mt 1:18-25)

This is how the birth of Jesus Christ came about [*after Mary returned from her three month stay in Judea*]: His mother Mary was pledged to be married to Joseph, but before they came together, she was found to be with child through the Holy Spirit. Because Joseph her husband was a righteous man and did not want to expose her to public disgrace, he had in mind to divorce her quietly.

But after he had considered this, an angel of the Lord appeared to him in a dream and said, "Joseph son of David, do not be afraid to take Mary home as your wife, because what is conceived in her is from the Holy Spirit. She will give birth to a son, and you are to give him the name Jesus, because he will save his people from their sins."

All this took place to fulfill what the Lord had said through the prophet: "The virgin will be with child and will give birth to a son, and they will call him **Immanuel**" – which means, "God with us."

When Joseph woke up, he did what the angel of the Lord had commanded him and took Mary home as his wife. But he had no union with her until she gave birth to a son.

[*As these events were taking place in Galilee, the following was happening in Judea*].

(Lk.1:57-80)

When it was time for Elizabeth to have her baby, she gave birth to a son. Her neighbors and relatives heard that the Lord had shown her great mercy, and they shared her joy.

On the eighth day they came to circumcise the child, and they were going to name him after his father Zechariah, but his mother spoke up and said, "No! He is to be called **John**."

They said to her, "There is no one among your relatives who has that name."

Then they made signs to his father, to find out what he would like to name the child. He asked for a writing tablet, and to everyone's astonishment he wrote, "His name is John." Immediately his mouth was opened and his tongue was loosed, and he began to speak, praising God. The neighbors were all filled with awe, and throughout the hill country of Judea people were talking about all these things. Everyone who heard this wondered about it, asking, "What then is this child going to be?" For the Lord's hand was with him.

His father Zechariah was filled with the Holy Spirit and prophesied:

"Praise be to the Lord, the God of Israel, because he has come and has redeemed his people.

He has raised up a horn of salvation for us in the house of his servant David.

(as he said through his holy prophets of long ago), salvation from our enemies and from the hand of all who hate us – to show mercy to our fathers and to remember his holy covenant, the oath he swore to our father Abraham: to rescue us from the hand of our enemies, and to enable us to serve him without fear in holiness and righteousness before him all our days." [*Since Mary had stayed in Zechariah's house for three months, he had known of the coming of the Savior, Jesus Christ. Therefore we find that he refers to His coming in the past tense.*]

"And you, my child, will be called a prophet of the Most High: for you will go on before the Lord to prepare the way for him, to give his people the knowledge of salvation through the forgiveness of their sins, because of the tender mercy of our God, by which the rising sun will come to us from heaven to shine on those living in darkness and in the shadow of death, to guide our feet into the path of peace."

And the child grew and became strong in spirit; and he lived in the desert until he appeared publicly to Israel.

II

BIRTH OF CHRIST

(Lk. 2:1-20)

In those days [*Nearly six months after the birth of John*], Caesar Augustus [*27B.C –14A.D*] issued a decree that a census should be taken of the entire Roman world. (This was the first census that took place while Quirinius was governor of Syria.) And everyone went to his own town to register.

So Joseph also went up from the town of Nazareth in Galilee to Judea, to Bethlehem the town of David, because he belonged to the house and line of David. He went there to register with Mary, who was pledged to be married to him and was expecting a child. While they were there, the time came for the baby to be born, and she gave birth to her firstborn[1], a son. She wrapped him in cloths and placed him in a manger, because there was no room for them in the inn.

And there were shepherds living out in the fields nearby, keeping watch over their flocks at night. An angel of the Lord appeared to them, and the glory of the Lord shone around them, and they were terrified. But the angel said to them, "Do not be afraid. I bring you good news of great joy that will be for all the people. Today[2] in the town of David a **Savior** has been born to you; he is **Christ the Lord**. This will be a sign to you: You will find a baby wrapped in cloths and lying in a manger."

Suddenly a great company of the heavenly host appeared with the angel, praising God and saying,

"Glory to God in the highest, and on earth peace to men on whom his favor rests."

When the angels had left them and gone into heaven, the shepherds said to one another, "Let's go to Bethlehem and see this thing that has happened, which the Lord has told us about."

So they hurried off and found Mary and Joseph, and the baby, who was lying in the manger. When they had seen him, they spread the word concerning what had been told them about this child, and all who heard it were amazed at what the shepherds said to them. But Mary treasured up all these things and pondered them in her heart.

The shepherds returned, glorifying and praising God for all the things they had heard and seen, which were just as they had been told.

(Mt. 1:1-17/ Lk. 3:23-38)

A record of the genealogy of Jesus Christ the son of David, the son of Abraham[3]

1	Abraham was the father of Isaac.	1	Joseph the son of Heli [4].
2	Isaac the father of Jacob	2	Heli the son of Matthat.
3	Jacob the father of Judah and his brothers.	3	Matthat the son of Levi.
4	Judah the father of Perez and Zerah whose mother was Tamar.	4	Levi the son of Melki.
5	Perez the father of Hezron.	5	Melki the son of Jannai.
6	Hezron the father of Ram	6	Jannai the son of Joseph.
7	Ram the father of Amminadab.	7	Joseph the son of Mattathias.
8	Amminadab the father of Nahshon.	8	Mattathias the son of Amos.
9	Nahshon the father of Salmon.	9	Amos the son of Nahum.
10	Salmon the father of Boaz, whose mother was Rahab.	10	Nahum the son of Esli.
11	Boaz the father of Obed, whose mother was Ruth.	11	Esli the son of Naggai.
12	Obed the father of Jesse.	12	Naggai the son of Maath.
13	Jesse the father of King David.	13	Maath the son of Mattathias
14	David was the father of Solomon, whose mother had been Uriah's wife.	14	Mattathias the son of Semein.
15	Solomon the father of Reheboam.	15	Semein the son of Josech.

16	Rehoboam the father of Abijah.	16	Josech the son of Joda.
17	Abijah the father of Asa.	17	Joda the son of Joanan.
18	Asa the father of Jehoshaphat.	18	Joanan the son of Rhesa.
19	Jehoshaphat the father of Jehoram.	19	Rhesa the son of Zerubbabel.
20	Jehoram the father of Uzziah[5].	20	Zerubbabel the son of Shealtiel[6].
21	Uzziah the father of Jotham.	21	Shealtiel the son of Neri[7].
22	Jotham the father of Ahaz.	22	Neri the son of Melki.
23	Ahaz the father of Hezekiah.	23	Melki the son of Addi.
24	Hezekiah the father of Manasseh.	24	Addi the son of Cosam.
25	Manasseh the father of Amon.	25	Cosam the son of Elmadam.
26	Amon the father of Josiah.	26	Elmadam the son of Er.
27	Josiah the father of Jeconiah and his brother sat the time of the exile to Babylon[8].	27	Er the son of Joshua.
28	After the exile to Babylon: Jeconiah was the father of Shealtiel.	28	Joshua the son of Eliezer.
29	Shealtiel the father of Zerubbabel.	29	Eliezer the son of Jorim.
30	Zerubbabel the father of Abiud.	30	Jorim the son of Matthat.
31	Abiud the father of Eliakim.	31	Matthat the son of Levi.
32	Eliakim the father of Azor.	32	Levi the son of Simeon.
33	Azor the father of Zadok.	33	Simeon the son of Judah.
34	Zadok the father of Akim.	34	Judah the son of Joseph.
35	Akim the father of Eliud.	35	Joseph the son of Jonam.
36	Eliud the father of Eleazar.	36	Jonam the son of Eliakim.
37	Eleazar the father of Matthan.	37	Eliakim the son of Melea.
38	Matthan the father of Jacob.	38	Melea the son of Menna.
39	Jacob the father of Joseph, the husband of Mary[9],	39	Menna the son of Mattatha.
40	of whom [] was born Jesus, who is called Christ.	40	Mattatha the son of Nathan.

41	Jesus	41	Nathan the son of David.
	Thus there were fourteen generations[10] in all from Abraham to David, fourteen from David to the exile to Babylon, and fourteen exile to the Christ.		
		42	David the son of Jesse.
		43	Jesse the son of Obed.
		44	Obed the son of Boaz.
		45	Boaz the son of from the Salmon.
		46	46. Salmon the son of Nahshon.
		47	Nahshon the son of Amminadab.
		48	Amminadab the son of Ram.
		49	Ram the son of Hezron.
		50	Hezron the son of Perez.
		51	Perez the son of Judah.
		52	Judah the son of Jacob.
		53	Jacob the son of Isaac.
		54	Isaac the son of Abraham
		55	Abraham the son of Terah.
		56	Terah the son of Nahor.
		57	Nahor the son of Serug.
		58	Serug the son of Reu.
		59	Reu the son of Peleg.
		60	Peleg the son of Eber.
		61	Eber the son of Shelah.
		62	Shelah the son of Cainan[11].
		63	Cainan the son ofArphaxad.
		64	Arphaxad the son of Shem.
		65	Shem the son of Noah.
		66	Noah the son of Lamech.
		67	Lamech the son of Methuselah.
		68	Methuselah the son of Enoch.
		69	Enoch the son of Jared.
		70	Jared the son of Mahalalel.
		71	Mahalalel the son of Kenan.
		72	Kenan the son of Enosh.
		73	Enosh the son of Seth.
		74	Seth the son of Adam.
		75	Adam the son of God.

(Lk. 2:21/Mt. 1:25)

On the eighth day, when it was time to circumcise him, he was named **Jesus**, the name the angel had given him before he had been conceived.

(Lk. 2:22-39)

When the time of their purification according to the Law of Moses had been completed Joseph and Mary took him [*from Bethlehem*] to Jerusalem to present him to the Lord (as it is written in the Law of the Lord, "Every first born male is to be consecrated to the Lord"), and to offer as sacrifice in keeping with what is said in the Law of the Lord: "a pair of doves or two young pigeons."

Now there was a man in Jerusalem called Simeon, who was righteous and devout. He was waiting for the consolation of Israel, and the Holy Spirit was upon him. It had been revealed to him by the Holy Spirit that he would not die before he had seen the Lord's Christ. Moved by the Spirit, he went into the temple courts. When the parents brought in the child Jesus to do for him what the custom of the Law required, Simeon took him in his arms and praised God, saying:

"Sovereign Lord, as you have promised,

you know dismiss your servant in peace.

For my eyes have seen your salvation,

which you have prepared in the sight of all people,

a light for revelation to the Gentiles

and for glory to your people Israel."

The child's father and mother marveled at what was said about him. Then Simeon blessed them and said to Mary, his mother: "This child is destined to cause the falling and rising of many in Israel, and to be a sign that will be spoken against, so that the thoughts of many hearts will be revealed. And a sword will pierce your own soul too."

There was also a prophetess, Anna, the daughter of Phanuel, of the tribe of Asher. She was very old; she had lived with her husband seven years after her marriage, and then was a widow until she was eighty-four. She never left the temple but worshiped night and day, fasting and praying. Coming up to them at that very moment, she gave thanks to God and spoke about the child to all who were looking forward to the redemption of Jerusalem.

When Joseph and Mary had done everything required by the Law of the Lord, they returned to Galilee to their own town of Nazareth.

STUDY NOTES

1. The couple was in the own town of Joseph. Why then should they lookout for an inn? Was there not a single relative in Joseph's own town for him to stay with? If they had looked out for an inn 'after the delivery' of the baby, where did the actual delivery take place? Probably by the roadside!

2. The shepherds were informed of the birth of Christ on the <u>very same day</u> of His birth.

3. When a person died without a son, Israelites had two ways of carrying on the particular person's name in their genealogies. They are as follows:

a) If that deceased person has a daughter and no son then the one who marries the daughter i.e., the son-in-law is considered as a legal son and is mentioned in the genealogy as a son.

b) If the deceased person has no issues at all then his brother is expected to marry the widow and bring forth a son to carry on his name. (Deut 25: 5-10) A son born this way is the actual son of the brother and legal son of the deceased person.

4. We find here that Luke refers to Heli as Joseph's father but at the same time we see Mathew mentioning Jacob as the father of Joseph. It is the considered opinion of biblical scholars that while Mathew gives Jesus' genealogy via his father Joseph, Luke gives the same genealogy through His mother Mary.

5. Jehoram was not the father of Uzziah.(II kings 8:24- 15:3)

Jehoram was the father of Ahaziah

Ahaziah was the father of Joash

Joash was the father of Amaziah

Amaziah was the father of Uzziah alias Azariah

Jehoram (880 – 841 B.C.) Ruled as a king from 848-841 B.C.

Ahaziah (863 – 841 B.C.) Ruled as a king 841 B.C.

Athaliah's reign 841-835 B.C.

Joash (842-796 B.C.) Ruled as a king from 835-796 B.C.

Amaziah(821-767 B.C.) Ruled as a king from 796-767 B.C.

Uzziah (806-739 B.C.) Ruled as a king from 790-739 B.C.

From the above it is clear that when Uzziah was born in 806B.C. It was 35 years since Jehoram had died. (841)!

6. Both Mathew and Luke in their genealogical accounts state that Shealtiel was the father of Zerubbabel. But when we read 1 Chr. 3:17-19 it is clear that Shealtiel had died without an issue and Pedaiah begat Zerubbabel, the legal son of Shealtiel (Mt. 1:12 / Lk. 3:7 / 1 Chr. 3:17-19).

7. Jeconiah was the father of Shealtiel, Shealtiel married the daughter of Neri who had no sons thus becoming Neri's legal son.

8. Josiah was not the father of Jeconiah (Please read 2 Kings 23:31-24:8) Josiah was the father of Jehoiakim alias Eliakim who was the father of Jeconiah alias Jehoiachin.

9. Jacob was the father of Joseph and Heli was the father-in-law of Joseph. Since Heli had no sons Joseph has been referred to as Heli's son in the genealogy.

10. When we consider the details from point no.5 stated above, it is obvious that the following statement is not true in the literal sense:

From Abraham to David – 14 generations

From David to the exile to Babylon – 14 generations

From the exile to the Christ – 14 generations

Total – 41 generations [Since David's name is mentioned twice, it is not 42 but 41]

Mathew is giving only the break up of 41 generations he has mentioned in his genealogical account and he is giving the correct genealogical route not the full genealogical details. From Abraham to Christ, Luke gives 56 generations, for the same period Mathew mentions of only 41 generations!

11. This name does not find any mention in the other genealogy lists in the Bible (Gen. 11:12-15 and 1 Chr. 1:24)

III

LIFE OF CHRIST TILL HE WAS THIRTY YEARS OLD

(Mt. 2:1-23)

After Jesus was born in Bethlehem in Judea, during the time of King Herod, Magi [*Traditionally wise men*] from the east came to Jerusalem and asked, "Where is the one who has been born king of the Jews? We saw his star in the east and have come to worship him." [*It is not stated here that the Magi were "three" in number*]

When king Herod heard this he was disturbed, and all Jerusalem with him. When he had called together all the people's chief priests and teachers of the law, he asked them where the Christ was to be born. "In Bethlehem in Judea," they replied, "For this is what the prophet has written:

"'But you, Bethlehem, in the land of Judah,

are by no means least among the rulers of Judah;

for out of you will come a ruler

who will be the shepherd of my people Israel.'"

Then Herod called the Magi secretly and found out from them the exact time the star had appeared. He sent them to Bethlehem and said, "Go and make a careful search for the child. As soon as you find him, report to me, so that I too may go and worship him."

After they had heard the king, they went on their way[1],and the star they had seen in the east went ahead of them until it stopped over the place where the child was. When they saw the star, they were overjoyed. On coming to the house, they saw the child with his mother Mary, and they bowed down and worshiped him. Then they opened their treasures and presented him with gifts of gold and of incense and the myrrh. And having been warned in a dream not to go back to Herod, they returned to their country by another route.

When they had gone, an angel of the Lord appeared to Joseph in a dream. "Get up," he said, "take the child and his mother and escape to Egypt. Stay there until I tell you, for Herod is going to search for the child to kill him[2]."

So he got up, took the child and his mother during the night and left for Egypt, where he stayed until the death of Herod. And so was fulfilled what the Lord had said through the prophet:

"Out of Egypt I called my son."

When Herod realized that he had been outwitted by the Magi, he was furious, and he gave orders to kill[3] all the boys in Bethlehem and its vicinity who were two years old and under, in accordance with the time he had learned from the Magi. Then what was said through the prophet Jeremiah was fulfilled:

"A voice is heard in Ramah[4],

weeping and great mourning,

Rachel weeping for her children

and refusing to be comforted,

because they are no more."

After Herod died [*1B.C*][5], an angel of the Lord appeared in a dream to Joseph in Egypt and said, "Get up, take the child and his mother and go to the land of Israel, for those who were trying to take the child's life are dead."

So he got up, took the child and his mother and went to the land of Israel. But when he heard that Archelaus [*1B.C-6A.D*] was reigning in Judea in place of his father Herod, he was afraid to go there. Having been warned in a dream, he withdrew to the district of Galilee, and he went and lived in a town called **Nazareth**. So was fulfilled what was said through the prophets: "He will be called a **Nazarene**."

(Lk. 2:40-52)

And the child grew and became strong; he was filled with wisdom, and the grace of God was upon him.

Every year his parents went to Jerusalem for the Feast of the Passover [*Celebrated around March / April*]. When he was twelve years old, they went up to the Feast, according to the custom. After the Feast was over, while his parents were returning home, the boy Jesus stayed behind in Jerusalem, but they were unaware of it. Thinking he was in their company, they traveled on for a day. Then they began looking for him among their relatives and friends. When they did not find him, they went back to Jerusalem to look for him. After three days they found him in the temple courts, sitting among the teachers, listening to them and asking them questions. Everyone who heard him was amazed at his understanding and his answers. When his parents saw him, they were astonished. His mother said to him, "Son, why have you treated us like this? Your father and I have been anxiously searching for you."

"Why were you searching for me?" he asked. "Didn't you know I had to be in my Father's house?" But they did not understand what he was saying to them.

Then he went down to Nazareth with them and was obedient to them. But his mother treasured all these things in her heart. And Jesus grew in wisdom and stature, and in favor with God and men.

STUDY NOTES

1. Did the Magi visit baby Jesus in the Bethlehem manger or in a house in Nazareth? Mt. 2: 9-11 does not specifically say that 'they went to Bethlehem' but says simply that 'they went on their way'. It is not fair to conclude that they had gone to Bethlehem when there is no such specific statement. Moreover, it must be noted that the Magi visited the child and its mother in a 'house' and not in a 'stable'.

When he was warned by the angel, Joseph left for Egypt that very same night itself and returns only after the death of Herod (Mt. 2:13-21). If the Magi had visited the child on the day of its birth itself - as the shepherds had done, it would mean that Joseph left that very night itself for Egypt 'from Bethlehem'. If it was so, then he could not have possibly gone to Jerusalem after forty days of the child's birth. More so because he purposely did not travel through Jerusalem on his return Journey (Mt. 2: 22,23). In this scenario, it is not possible to accommodate the events narrated in Lk.2:21-39. Luke explicitly says that Joseph had taken baby Jesus 'from Bethlehem to Jerusalem' after forty days of its birth and then, 'from here proceeded to Nazareth'.

When Luke's account is given precedence over Mathew's in the chronological order of the events, we get a clear picture of the events related to the birth of Christ.

From this chronology, it is understood that the Magi's visit was at least forty days after the birth of the child. Since Herod ordered the execution of children below two years, this gap could even be few months! We understand that the Magi were directed by Herod (As per the Pharisees' advise) from 'Jerusalem to Bethlehem' but they were instead led from 'Jerusalem to Nazareth' (by the star).

Therefore we conclude that the Magi unlike the shepherds, had visited the child and its mother in a house in Nazareth after at least a few months of its birth and not in the Bethlehem manger on the day of its birth.

2. This is the first unsuccessful attempt to kill Jesus.

Second unsuccessful attempt Chapter 13 Study Note No: 1

Third unsuccessful attempt Chapter 19 Study Note No: 4

Fourth unsuccessful attempt Chapter 19 Study Note No: 8

3. Joseph is being warned well before the order to kill was actually given. By the time order for the massacre was given, the baby which had already been taken from Bethlehem to Nazareth, was now taken from there to Egypt upon the angel's warning - well before the massacre could even begin!

4. If Ramah that is 7.5 miles (approx) from Bethlehem was within the radius of the massacre, then Jerusalem which is only 3.7 miles (approx) from Bethlehem should also have been included in this pogrom.

5. Dating the birth of Christ:

The birth of Jesus Christ is a defining moment in the history of mankind. Quitefittingly the birth of Christ divides history into Pre and Post Eras of Christ. Experts do differ in their opinion regarding the exact year of Christ's birth. Majority of the bible scholars hold the view that the birth of Christ should have been on or before 4 B.C.

This is because Herod the great, who tried to kill Jesus as a child, is thought to have died in the year- 4 B.C. We are unable to subscribe to this view because, the birth of Christ in 4 B.C does not corroborate with Lk. 3:1 which states that John began his ministry in the 15th year of Tiberius Caesar i.e., 28 A.D. This means that Jesus who was baptized by John must have been baptized on or after 28 A.D. Jesus was 30 years old when he was baptized. This tells us that the birth of Christ should have been on or after 2 B.C only.

There is a school of thought which in an attempt to explain Lk.3:1, says that Luke had calculated the fifteen years from the years of Tiberius Caesar's co-regency with his father rather than from his year of accession

(14 AD).

Yes it is indeed true that Tiberius Caesar had been a co- regent with his father Augustus before he became an emperor himself. Tiberius Caesar became a co-regent to his father in 13 A.D. Even if calculated from his year of co-regency, 15th year- the beginning of John's ministry would be either 27 or 28 AD. This would put the birth of Christ who was 30 years old when baptized at 3 or 2 BC and certainly not 4 BC as supposed to be!

More over, there is no clear evidence to say that Luke had made his calculations from 13 AD. Therefore there is no reason to assume the same. That being the case we have to take Lk.3: 1 by its face value i.e., that Luke had calculated from year of accession of Tiberius Caesar (14 AD) which means his fifteenth year is 28/29 AD. Calculating from this date it is an obvious conclusion that Christ's birth was not before 2 BC.

The natural question now is, did then Herod the great die before the birth of Christ i.e. in 4 B.C? Those chronologists who suggest this date, are based to a large extent on Josephus' history. In the same historian's account, there are enough references to suggest that the death of Herod the great could have occurred in 2 or 1 A.D. They are as follows:

1. According to Josephus, Herod died not long after an eclipse of the moon and before a Passover. (*Jewish Antiquities, XVII*, 167[vi, 4]; 213[ix, 3]) Since there was an eclipse on March 13, 4 BC. (March 13, Julian), some have concluded that this was the eclipse referred to by Josephus. ("Lewis Foster" *T. Exp. B.C NIV,*" *Vol.,* 1.Pg 595). On the other hand there was an <u>eclipse of the moon in 1 BC also</u>, about three months before the Passover, <u>while the one in 4 BC was only partial</u>, this was a TOTAL ECLIPSE! Josephus' account could have meant the latter rather than the former. (*Wikipedia, the free encyclopedia*- Herod the great –His death).

2. Another line of calculation centers on the age Herod at the time of his death. Josephus says he was 70 years old. He says that at the time Herod received his appointment as governor of Galilee (which is generally dated as 47 BC.), when he was 15 years old; but this has been understood by scholars to be an error, 25 years evidently being intended. (*Jewish Antiquities, XVII*, 148[vi, 1]; XIV, 158[ix, 2]) Accordingly, Herod's death occurred 2 BC or 1 BC. (*Wikipedia, the free encyclopedia*- Herod the great –His death)

3. Josephus places Herod's capture of Jerusalem in 37 BC, but he also says that this occurred 27 years after the capture of the city by Pompey (which

was in 63 BC) (*Jewish Antiquities, XIV,* 487,488[xvi, 4]). His reference to that later event would make the date of Herod's taking the city of Jerusalem 36 BC. Now Josephus says that Herod died 37 years from the time that he was appointed king by the Romans and 34 years after he took Jerusalem. (*Jewish Antiquities, XVI,* 190,191[viii, 1]) This might indicate that the date of his death was 2 BC or perhaps 1 BC. (*Wikipedia, the free encyclopedia*- Herod the great –His death)

Therefore from the above-stated details it can be deducted that **Christ was born in 2 BC** and **Herod the Great died in 1 BC** – after the birth of Christ. This conclusion is biblical and at the same time historically not incorrect.

MINISTRY OF JESUS CHRIST

IV

JOHN THE BAPTIST

(Mt. 3:1-3 / Mk. 1:2-4 / Lk. 3:1-6)
In the fifteenth year [*28/29 A.D.*] of the reign of Tiberius Caesar [*14 – 37 A.D.*] when,

Pontius Pilate was the Governor Of Judea
Herod was the Tetrarch Of Galilee
Herod's brother Philip was the Tetrarch Of Iturea and Traconitis
Lysanias was the Tetrach of Abilene

during the high priesthood of Annas and Caiaphas, the word of God came to John son of Zechariah in the desert. He went into all the country around the Jordan, preaching a baptism[1] of repentance for the forgiveness of sins. As is written in the book of the words of Isaiah the prophet:

- "I will send my messenger ahead of you, who will prepare your way."
- "A voice of one calling in the desert, 'prepare the way for the Lord, makes straight paths for him.
- Every valley shall be filled in, every mountain and hill made low. The crooked roads shall become straight, the rough ways smooth.
- And all mankind will see God's salvation.' "

In those days John the Baptist came, preaching in the Desert of Judea and saying, "Repent, for the kingdom of heaven is near." This is he who was spoken of through the prophet Isaiah.

(Mt. 3:4 / Mk. 1:6)

John's clothes were made of camel's hair, and he had a leather belt around his waist. His food was locusts and wild honey.

(Mt. 3:5,6 / Mk. 1:5)

People went out to him from Jerusalem and all Judea and the whole region of Jordan. Confessing their sins, they were baptized by him in the Jordan River.

(Mt. 3:7-10 / Lk. 3:7-9)

But when he saw many of the Pharisees and Sadducees coming to where he was baptizing, he said to them, "You brood of vipers! Who warned you to flee from the coming wrath? Produce fruit in keeping with repentance. And do not think you can say to yourselves, 'We have Abraham as our father.' I tell you that out of these stones God can raise up children for Abraham. The ax is already at the root of the trees, and every tree that does not produce good fruit will be cut down and thrown into the fire."

(Lk. 3:10-14)

"What should we do then?" the crowd asked.

John answered, "The man with two tunics should share with him who has none, and the one who has food should do the same."

Tax collectors also came to be baptized. "Teacher," they asked, "what should we do?"

"Don't collect any more than you are required to," he told them.

Then some soldiers asked him, "And what should we do?"

He replied, "Don't extort money and don't accuse people falsely – be content with your pay."

(Mt. 3: 13-17 / Mk. 1: 9-11 / Lk. 3: 21-23)

When all the people were being baptized, Jesus came from Nazareth in Galilee to the Jordan to be baptized byJohn[2]. But John tried to deter[3] him saying, "I need to be baptized by you, and do you come to me?"

Jesus replied, "Let it be so now. It is proper for us to do this to fulfill all righteousness." Then John consented and Jesus was baptized by John in Jordan.

As soon as Jesus was baptized he went up out of the water and as he was praying, he saw heaven being torn open and the Spirit descending on him like a dove. And a voice came from heaven[3], "You are my son, whom I love; with you I am well pleased." Now Jesus himself was about thirty years old when he began his ministry.

(Mt. 4:1-11 / Mk. 1:12,13 / Lk. 4:1-13)

Jesus full of the Holy Spirit returned from the Jordan and was led by the Spirit into the desert to be tempted by the devil where for forty days he was tempted by the devil. He was with the wild animals. He ate nothing during those days and at the end of them he was hungry[4].

The devil, the tempter said to him, "If you are the Son of God, tell these stones to become bread." Jesus answered, "It is written: 'Man does not live on bread alone, but on every word that comes from the mouth of God.'

"The devil led him up to a high place and showed him in an instant all the kingdoms of the world. And he said to him, "I will give you all their authority and splendor, for it has been given to me, and I can give it to any one I want to. So if you worship me, it will all be yours."

Jesus said to him, "Away from me Satan! For it is written: 'Worship the Lord your God and serve him only.'

"The devil led him to Jerusalem and had him stand on the highest point of the temple. "If you are the Son of God," he said, "Throw yourself down from here. For it is written:

'He will command his angels concerning you to guard you carefully; they will lift you up in their hands, so that you will not strike your foot against a stone.'

"Jesus answered him, "It is also written: 'Do not put the Lord your God to test.'"

When the devil had finished all this tempting, he left him until an opportune time and angels came and attended him.

[*As Jesus' days of temptations were in progress, the following happened near Jordan i.e., 39/38th day*]

(Mt. 3:11,12 / Mk. 1:7,8 / Lk. 3:15-18 / Jn. 1:19-28)

[*When*] The people were waiting expectantly and were all wondering in their hearts if John might possibly be the Christ, this was John's testimony when the Jews of Jerusalem sent priests and Levites to ask him who he was. He did not fail to confess but confessed freely, "I am not the Christ."

They asked him, "Then who are you? Are you Elijah?"

He said, "I am not."

"Are you the prophet?"

He answered, "No"

Finally they said, "Who are you? Give us an answer to take back to those who sent us. What do you say about yourself?"

John replied in the words of Isaiah the prophet, "I am the voice of one calling in the desert, 'Make straight the way for the Lord.'

"Now some Pharisees who had been sent questioned him, "Why then do you baptize if you are not the Christ, or Elijah, nor the prophet?"

"I baptize with water," John replied, "But among you stands one more powerful than I, you do not know. He is the one who comes after me, the thongs of whose sandals I am not worthy to stoop down and untie. He will baptize you with the Holy Spirit and with fire. His winnowing fork is in his hand to clear his threshing floor and to gather the wheat in his barn, but he will burn up the chaff with unquenchable fire." And with many other words John exhorted the people and preached the good news to them.

(Jn. 1: 29-42)

[After being tested by the devil for forty days, Jesus comes back to Jordan]

The next day John saw Jesus coming toward him and said, "Look, the Lamb of God, who takes away the sin of the world! This is the one I meant when I said, 'A man who comes after me has surpassed me because he was before me.' I myself did not know him, but the reason I came baptizing with water was that he might be revealed to Israel."

Then John gave this testimony: "I saw the Spirit comedown from heaven as a dove and remain on him, I would not have known him, except that the one who sent me to baptize with water told me. 'The man on whom you see the Spirit come down and remain is he who will baptize with the Holy Spirit.' I have seen and I testify that this is the Son of God."

The next day John was there again with two of his disciples. When he saw Jesus passing by, he said, "Look, the Lamb of God!"

When the two disciples heard him say this, they followed Jesus. Turning around, Jesus saw them following and asked, "What do you want?"

They said, "Rabbi" (which means Teacher), "where are you staying?"

"Come", he replied, "and you will see."

So they went and saw where he was staying, and spent that day with him. It was about the tenth hour.

Andrew, Simon Peter's brother, was one of the two who heard what John had said and who had followed Jesus. The first thing Andrew did was to find his brother Simon and tell him, "We have found the Messiah" (that is, the Christ). And he brought him to Jesus.

Jesus looked at him and said, "Your are Simon son of John. You will be called Cephas" (which, when translated, is Peter).

STUDY NOTES

1. The word 'baptism' is mentioned for the first time.

2. The baptism of Jesus Christ is an event that is narrated by all the four Gospel writers.

3. When Jesus came to be baptized, John deters Jesus before He was actually baptized. In the crowd that came to be baptized how did John recognize Jesus as the Christ? The reason John came baptizing with water was that Christ might be revealed to Israel (Jn. 1:31). And Jn.1:32&33 gives us the identity John was given to identify the Christ. But according to the sequence of events given in Mt. 3:13-17 it was only after Jesus Christ was baptized and came out of water, did the Holy Sprit descend on Him. This being the case how then did John recognize Him as the Christ even before the baptism itself?

The explanation is as follows:

A closer reading of the scriptures reveals that before the baptism, it was John who 'saw' (Jn.1: 34) and after the baptism, it was Jesus who 'saw' (Mt. 3:16). Therefore John should have seen it as a vision before the actual event, while Jesus saw the same- also as a vision after the baptism. But when Mt. 3:17 states simply that 'a voice came from heaven', it can be inferred that the voice was audible to all those present including John, Jesus and all people around. Also note that John's vision did not include the voice from heaven.

This is the first of the three times a voice from heaven was heard during Christ's Ministry. The other two are:

a. Chapter 18 Study Note No: 2

b. Chapter 27 Study Note No: 9

4. By this we understand that the following three temptations were at the end of forty days of temptations and fasting.

V

THE BEGINNING OF CHRIST'S MINISTRY

(Jn. 1:43-2:12)

The next day Jesus decided to leave for Galilee. Finding Philip, he said to him, "Follow me."

Philip, like Andrew and Peter, was from the town of Bethsaida. Philip found Nathanael and told him, "We have found the one Moses wrote about in the Law, and about whom the prophets also wrote – Jesus of Nazareth, the son of Joseph."

"Nazareth! Can anything good come from there?" Nathanael asked.

"Come and see," said Philip.

When Jesus saw Nathanael approaching, he said of him, "Here is a true Israelite, in whom there is nothing false."

"How do you know me?" Nathanael asked.

Jesus answered, "I saw you while you were still under the fig tree before Philip called you."

Then Nathanael declared, "Rabbi, you are the Son of God; you are the King of Israel."

Jesus said, "Do you believe because I told you I saw you under the fig tree? You shall see greater things than that," He then added, "I tell you the truth, you shall see heaven open, and the angels of God ascending and descending on the Son of Man."

On the third day [*six days after the forty-day temptation*] a wedding took place at Cana in Galilee. Jesus' mother was there, and Jesus and his disciples had also been invited to the wedding. When the wine was gone, Jesus' mother said to him, "They have no more wine."

"Dear woman, why do you involve me?" Jesus replied. "My time has not yet come."

His mother said to the servants, "Do whatever he tells you."

Nearby stood six stone water jars, the kind used by the Jews for ceremonial washing, each holding from twenty to thirty gallons.

Jesus said to the servants, "Fill the jars with water"; so they filled them to the brim.

Then he told them, "Now draw some out and take it to the master of the banquet."

They did so, and the master of the banquet tasted the water that had been turned into wine. He did not realize where it had come from, though the servants who had drawn the water knew. Then he called the bridegroom aside and said, "Everyone brings out the choice wine first and then the cheaper wine after the guests have had too much to drink; but you have saved the best till now."

This, the first of his miraculous signs, Jesus performed in Cana of Galilee. He thus revealed his glory, and his disciples put their faith in him.

After this he went down to Capernaum with his mother and brothers and his disciples. There they stayed for a few days.

(Jn. 2:13, 23-3:36)

When it was almost time for the Jewish Passover, Jesus went up to Jerusalem[1]. Now while he was in Jerusalem at the Passover Feast, many people saw the miraculous signs he was doing and believed in his name. But Jesus would not entrust himself to them, for he knew all men. He did not need man's testimony about man, for he knew what was in a man.

Now there was a man of the Pharisees named Nicodemus, a member of the Jewish ruling council. He came to Jesus at night and said, "Rabbi, we know you are a teacher who has come from God. For no one could perform the miraculous signs you are doing if God were not with him."

In reply Jesus declared, "I tell you the truth, no one can see the kingdom of God unless he is born again."

"How can a man be born when he is old?" Nicodemus asked. "Surely he cannot enter a second time into his mother's womb to be born!"

Jesus answered, "I tell you the truth, no one can enter the kingdom of God unless he is born of water and the Spirit. Flesh gives birth to flesh, but the Spirit gives birth to spirit. You should not be surprised at my saying, 'You must be born again.' The wind blows wherever it pleases. You hear its sound, but you cannot tell where it comes from or where it is going. So it is with everyone born of the Spirit."

"How can this be?" Nicodemus asked.

"You are Israel's teacher," said Jesus, "and do you not understand these things? I tell you the truth we speak of what we know, and we testify to what we have seen, but still you people do not accept our testimony. I have spoken to you of earthly things and you do not believe; how then will you believe if I speak of heavenly things? No one has ever gone into heaven except the one who came from heaven – the Son of Man. Just as Moses lifted up the snake in the desert, so the Son of Man must be lifted up[2], that everyone who believes in him may have eternal life.

"For God so loved the world that he gave his only begotten Son, that whoever believes in him shall not perish but have eternal life. For God did not send his Son into the world to condemn the world, but to save the world through him. Whoever believes in him is not condemned, but whoever does not believe stands condemned already because he has not believed in the name of God's only begotten Son. This is the verdict: Light has come into the world, but men loved darkness instead of light because their deeds were evil. Everyone who does evil hates the light, and will not come into the light for fear that his deeds will be exposed. But whoever lives by the truth comes into the light, so that it may be seen plainly that what he has done has been done through God."

After this, Jesus and his disciples went out into the Judean countryside, where he spent some time with them and baptized. Now John also was baptizing at Aenon near Salim, because there was plenty of water, and people were constantly coming to be baptized. (This was before John was put in prison.) An argument developed between some of John's disciples and a certain Jews over the matter of ceremonial washing. They came to John and said to him, "Rabbi, that man who was with you on the other side of the Jordan – the one you testified about – well, he is baptizing, and everyone is going to him."

To this John replied, "A man can receive only what is given him from heaven. You yourselves can testify that I said, 'I am not the Christ but am sent ahead of him.' The bride belongs to the bridegroom. The friend who attends the bridegroom waits and listens for him, and is full of joy when he hears the bridegroom's voice. That joy is mine, and it is now complete. He must become greater; I must become less.

"The one who comes from above is above all; the one who is from the earth belongs to the earth, and speaks as one from the earth. The one who comes from heaven is above all. He testifies to what he has seen and heard, but no one accepts his testimony. The man who has accepted it has certified that God is truthful. For the one whom God has sent speaks the words of God, for God gives the Spirit without limit. The Father loves the Son and has placed everything in his hands. Whoever believes in the Son has eternal life, but whoever rejects the Son will not see life, for God's wrath remains on him."

(Mt. 14:3-5 / Mk. 6:17,18 / Lk. 3:19,20)

Herod had arrested John and bound him and put him in prison because of Herodias, his brother Philip's wife, for John had been saying to him: "It is not lawful for you to have her." Herod wanted to kill John, but he was afraid of the people, because they considered him a prophet.

Thus, because of Herodias, his brother's wife, and all the other evil things he had done, Herod added this to them all: He locked John up in prison[3].

(Mt. 4:12 / Mk. 1:14 / Lk. 4:14 / Jn. 4:1-3)

The Pharisees heard that Jesus was gaining and baptizing more disciples than John, although in fact it was not Jesus who baptized, but his disciples. When the Lord learned of this and heard that John had been put in prison, he left Judea[4] and returned once more to Galilee in the power of the Spirit.

(Jn. 4:4-43)

Now he had to go through Samaria. So he came to a town in Samaria called Sychar, near the plot of ground Jacob had given to his son Joseph. Jacob's well was there, and Jesus, tired as he was from the journey, sat down by the well. It was about the sixth hour.

When a Samaritan woman came to draw water, Jesus said to her, "Will you give me a drink?" (His disciples had gone into the town to buy food.)

The Samaritan woman said to him, "You are a Jew and I am a Samaritan woman. How can you ask me for a drink?" (For Jews do not associate with Samaritans.)

Jesus answered her, "If you knew the gift of God and who it is that asks you for a drink, you would have asked him and he would have given you living water."

"Sir," the woman said, "you have nothing to draw with and the well is deep. Where can you get this living water? Are you greater than our father Jacob, who gave us the well and drank from it himself, as did also his sons and his flocks and herds?"

Jesus answered, "Everyone who drinks this water will be thirsty again, but whoever drinks the water I give him will never thirst. Indeed, the water I give him will become in him a spring of water welling up to eternal life."

The woman said to him, "Sir, give me this water so that I won't get thirsty and have to keep coming here to draw water."

He told her, "Go, call your husband and come back."

"I have no husband," she replied.

Jesus said to her, "You are right when you say you have no husband. The fact is, you have had five husbands, and the man you now have is not your husband. What you have just said is quite true."

"Sir," the woman said, "I can see that you are a prophet. Our fathers worshiped on this mountain, but you Jews claim that the place where we must worship is in Jerusalem."

Jesus declared, "Believe me, woman, a time is coming when you will worship the Father neither on this mountain nor in Jerusalem. You Samaritans worship what you do not know; we worship what we do know, for salvation is from the Jews. Yet a time is coming and has now come when the true worshipers will worship the Father in spirit and truth, for they are the kind of worshipers the Father seeks. God is spirit, and his worshipers must worship in spirit and in truth."

The woman said, "I know that Messiah "(calledChrist)" is coming. When he comes, he will explain everything to us."

Then Jesus declared, "I who speak to you am he."

Just then his disciples returned and were surprised to find him talking with a woman. But no one asked, "What do you want?" or "Why are you talking with her?"

Then, leaving her water jar, the woman went back to the town and said to the people, "Come, see a man who told me everything I ever did. Could this be the Christ?" They came out of the town and made their way toward him.

Meanwhile his disciples urged him, "Rabbi, eat something."

But he said to them,: I have food to eat that you know nothing about."

Then his disciples said to each other, "Could someone have brought him food?"

"My food," said Jesus, "is to do the will of him who sent me and to finish his work. Do you not say, 'Four months more and then the harvest'? I tell you, open your eyes and look at the fields! They are ripe for harvest. Even now the reaper draws his wages, even now he harvests the crop for eternal life, so that the sower and the reaper may be glad together. Thus the saying 'One sows and another reaps' is true. I sent you to reap what you have not worked for. Others have done the hard work, and you have reaped the benefits of their labor."

Many of the Samaritans from that town believed in him because of the woman's testimony, "He told me everything I ever did." So when the Samaritans came to him, they urged him to stay with them, and he stayed two days. And because of his words many more became believers.

They said to the woman, "We no longer believe just because of what you said; now we have heard for ourselves, and we know that this man really is the Savior of the world."

After the two days he left for Galilee.

STUDY NOTES

1. The author of John's Gospel gives a picture that it was on the first Passover festival during Jesus' Ministry that the cleansing of the temple had taken place. But when the same is seen in the light of other three Gospels put together it becomes clear that the said event had taken place only on the fourth and last Passover festival. There are a few scholars who believe that there were two incidents of temple cleansing. This is highly unlikely because the sign that Jesus gave when the Jews demanded one, is something that Jesus started taking only during the fag end of His ministry (His body – temple – third day resurrection). Moreover John does not repeat another incident of the same kind in the fourth Passover. Hence it can be safely concluded that there was only one incident of temple cleansing and that was on the fourth Passover only.

Second Passover Chapter 8 Study Note No.:1

Third Passover Chapter 16 Study Note No.:3

Fourth Passover Chapter 22 Study Note No.:2

2. Jesus talks about the same thing again in Chapter 25 Study Note No.: 10

3. John and Jesus were both ministering at the same time near Jordan when Herod was doing evil things. Probably since Jesus did not speak

against those evil deeds, Herod had arrested only John - the one who had spoken.

4. John's imprisonment and the Pharisees coming to know of His growing ministry were the two reasons Jesus shifted His ministerial base from Judea to Galilee.

VI

MINISTRY'S BASE SHIFTED TO GALILEE

(Jn. 4: 44-54)

(Now Jesus himself had pointed out that a prophet has no honor in his own country.) When he arrived in Galilee, the Galileans welcomed him. They had seen all that he had done in Jerusalem at the Passover Feast, for they also had been there.

Once more he visited Cana in Galilee, where he had turned the water into wine. And there was a certain royal official whose son lay sick at Capernaum. When this man heard that Jesus had arrived in Galilee from Judea, he went to him and begged him to come and heal his son, who was close to death.

"Unless you people see miraculous signs and wonders," Jesus told him, "You will never believe."

The royal official said, "Sir, come down before my child dies."

Jesus replied, "You may go. Your son will live."

The man took Jesus at his word and departed. While he was still on the way, his servants met him with the news that his boy was living. When he inquired as to the time when his son got better, they said to him, "The fever left him yesterday at the seventh hour."

Then the father realized that this was the exact time at which Jesus had said to him, "Your son will live." So he and all his household believed.

This was the second miraculous sign that Jesus performed, having come from Judea to Galilee. [*The first miracle was also performed in Cana, Galilee.*]

(Mt. 4:13-17 / Mk. 1:14,15)

Leaving Nazareth, Jesus went and lived in Capernaum, which was by the lake in the area of Zebulun and Naphtali – to fulfill what was said through the prophet Isaiah:

"Land of Zebulun and land of Naphtali,

the way to the sea, along the Jordan,

Galilee of the Gentiles –

the people living in darkness

have seen a great light;

on those living in the land of the shadow of

death a light was dawned."

Thus Jesus went into Galilee, proclaiming the good news of God. "The time has come," Jesus began to Preach, "The kingdom of God is near, Repent and believe the good news!"

(Mt. 4:18-22 / Mk. 1:16-20 / Lk. 5: 1-11)

One day as Jesus as standing by the Lake of Gennesaret, (*Probably early morning*) with the people crowding around him and listening to the word of God, he saw at the water's edge two boats, left there by the fishermen, who were washing their nets. He got into one of the boats, the one belonging to Simon, and asked him to put out a little from shore. Then he sat down and taught the people from the boat.

When he finished speaking, he said to Simon, "Put out into deep water, and let down the nets for a catch."

Simon answered, "Master, we've worked hard all night and haven't caught anything. But because you say so, I will let down the nets."

When they had done so, they caught such a large number of fish that their nets began to break. So they signaled their partners in the other boat to come and help them, and they came and filled both boats so full that they began to sink.

When Simon Peter saw this, he fell at Jesus' knees and said, "Go away from me, Lord; I am a sinful man!" For he and all his companions were astonished at the catch of fish they had taken, and so were James and John, the sons of Zebedee, Simon's partners.

Then Jesus said to Simon, "Don't be afraid; from now on you will catch men." So they pulled their boats up on shore, left everything and followed him.

(Mt. 4:23-25, 8:14-17 / Mk. 1:21-39 / Lk. 4:15, 31-44)

They went to Capernaum, and when the Sabbath came, Jesus went into the synagogue and began to teach. The people were amazed at his teaching, because he taught them as one who had authority, not as the teachers of the law. Just then a man in their synagogue who was possessed by an evil spirit cried out, "What do you want with us, Jesus of Nazareth? Have you come to destroy us? I know who you are – the Holy One of God!"

"Be quiet!" said Jesus sternly. "Come out of him!" The evil spirit shook the man violently and came out of him with a shriek.

The people were all so amazed that they asked each other, "What is this? A new teaching – and with authority! He even gives orders to evil spirits and they obey him." News about him spread quickly over the whole region of Galilee.

As soon as they left the synagogue, they went with James and John to the home of Simon and Andrew. Simon's mother-in-law was in bed with a high fever, and they told Jesus about her. So he went to her, took her hand and helped her up. The fever left her and she began to wait on them.

That evening after sunset the people brought to Jesus all the sick and demon-possessed. The whole town gathered at the door, and Jesus healed many who had various diseases. He also drove out many demons with a word. Demons came out of many people shouting, "You are the Son of God!" But he would not let the demons speak because they knew who he was.

This was to fulfill what was spoken through the prophet Isaiah:

"He took up our infirmities and carried our diseases."

Very early in the morning, while it was still dark, Jesus got up, left the house and went off to a solitary place, where he prayed. Simon and his companions went to look for him, and when they found him, they exclaimed: "Everyone is looking for you!" and they tried to keep him from leaving them.

Jesus replied, "Let us go somewhere else – to the nearby villages – so I can preach there also. That is why I have come."

Jesus went throughout Galilee, teaching in their synagogues, preaching the good news of the kingdom, and healing every disease and sickness among the people and driving out demons and every one praised him.

News about him spread all over Syria, and people brought to him all who were ill with various disease, those suffering severe pain, the demon-possessed, those having seizures, and the paralyzed, and he healed them. Large crowds from Galilee, the Decapolis, Jerusalem, Judea and the region across the Jordan followed him.

(Mt. 9:2-8 / Mk. 2:1-12 / Lk. 5:17-26)

A few days later, when Jesus again entered Capernaum, the people heard that he had come home. So many gathered that there was no room left, not even outside the door, and he preached the word to them. As he was teaching, Pharisees and teachers of the law, who had come from every village of Galilee and from Judea and Jerusalem, were sitting there[1]. And the power of the Lord was present for him to heal the sick.

Some men came, bringing to him a paralytic, carried by four of them. They tried to take him into the house to lay him before Jesus. When they could not find a way to do this because of the crowd, they went up on the roof made on opening in the roof above Jesus and lowered him on his mat through the tiles into the middle of the crowd, right in front of Jesus.

When Jesus saw their faith, he said, "Take heart Son, your sins are forgiven."

The Pharisees and the teachers of the law began thinking to themselves, "Who is this fellow who speaks blasphemy? Who can forgive sins but God alone?"

Immediately Jesus knew in his spirit that this was what they were thinking in their hearts, and he said to them, "Why are you thinking these evil thoughts in your hearts which is easier: to say to the paralytic, 'Your sins are forgiven,' or to say, 'Get up, take your mat and walk'? But that you may know that the Son of Man has authority on earth to forgive sins...." He said to the paralytic, "I tell you, get up, take your mat and go home." Immediately he stood up in front of them took his mat and in full view of them all went home praising God. Everyone was amazed saying, "We have never seen anything like this!" and they praised God, who had given such authority to men. They were filled with awe and said, "We have seen remarkable things today."

(Mt. 9:9-17 / Mk. 2:13-22 / Lk. 5:27-39)

Once again Jesus went out beside the lake. A large crowd came to him, and he began to teach them. As walked along, he saw Levi [*Mathew*] son of Alphaeus sitting at the tax collector's booth. "Follow me," Jesus told him, and Levi got up left everything and followed him.

Then Levi held a great banquet for Jesus at his house, many tax collectors and "sinners" were eating with him and his disciples. But the Pharisees and the teachers of the law who belonged to their sect complained to his disciples, "Why does your teacher eat with tax collectors and 'sinners'?"

On hearing this, Jesus said, "It is not the healthy who need a doctor, but the sick. But go and learn what this means: 'I desire mercy, not sacrifice.' For I have not come to call the righteous, but sinners."

Now John's disciples and the Pharisees were fasting. John's disciples came and asked him, "How is it that we and the Pharisees fast, but your disciples do not fast?"

Jesus answered, "How can the guests of the bridegroom mourn while he is with them? They cannot so long as they have him with them. The time will come when the bridegroom will be taken from them, then they will fast."

He told them this parable: "No one sews a patch of unshrunk cloth on an old garment, for the patch will pull away from the garment, making the tear worse. And the patch from the new will not match the old. Neither do men pour new wine into old wineskins. If they do, the skins will burst, the wine will run out and the wineskins will be ruined. No, they pour new wine into new wineskins, and both are preserved. And no one after drinking old wine wants the new, for he says, 'The old is better'."

STUDY NOTES

1. The return of Jesus and such a large gathering, consisting of religious leaders from a wide area, assembling here on that very same day, seems more than a coincidence. It is more probable that they are a team sent to enquire Jesus about His ministry- the same way they had enquired John in the past. They may have in fact summoned Jesus from His ministerial tour for this purpose. Jesus uses this opportunity provided to Him to **PROVE** them that He was **THE SON OF MAN** and that **He had the authority to forgive sins** – the result was that they went back filled with awe!
There were totally three such missions sent by the religious leaders. The others are as follows:
Chapter 10 Study Note No: 4
Chapter 17 Study Note No: 3

VII

CHRIST IN JERUSALEM

(Jn. 5: 1-47)

Some time later, Jesus went up to Jerusalem for a feast of the Jews [*Could be the feast of Tabernacles celebrated around September/ October*][1]. Now there is in Jerusalem near the Sheep Gate a pool, which in Aramaic is called Bethesda and which is surrounded by five covered colonnades. Here a great number of disabled people used to lie-the blind, the lame, the paralyzed and they waited for the moving of the waters. From time to time an angel of the Lord would comedown and stir the waters. The first one into the pool after each such disturbance would be cured of whatever disease he had. One who was there had been an invalid for thirty-eight years. When Jesus saw him lying there and learned that he had been in this condition for a long time, he asked him, "Do you want to get well?"

"Sir," the invalid replied, "I have no one to help me into the pool when the water is stirred. While I am trying to get in, someone else goes down ahead of me."

Then Jesus said to him, "Get up! Pick up your mat and walk." At once the man was cured; he picked up his mat and walked.

The day on which this took place was a Sabbath, and so the Jews said to the man who had been healed, "It is the Sabbath; the law forbids you to carry your mat."

But he replied, "The man who made me well said to me, 'Pick up your mat and walk.' "So they asked him, "Who is this fellow who told you to pick it up and walk?"

The man who was healed had no idea who it was, for Jesus had slipped away into the crowd that was there.

Later Jesus found him at the temple and said to him, "See, you are well again. Stop sinning or something worse may happen to you." The man went away and told the Jews that it was Jesus who had made him well[2].

So, because Jesus was doing these things on the Sabbath, the Jews persecuted him. Jesus said to them, "My father is always at his work to this very day, and I, too, am working." For this reason the Jews tried all the harder to kill him; not only was he breaking the Sabbath, but he was even calling God his own Father, making himself equal with God.

Jesus gave them this answer: "I tell you the truth, the Son can do nothing by himself; he can do only what he sees his Father doing, because whatever the Father does the Son also does. For the Father loves the Son and shows him all he does. Yes, to your amazement he will show him even greater things than these. For just as the Father raises the dead and gives them life, even so the Son gives life to whom he is pleased to give it. Moreover, the Father judges no one, but has entrusted all judgment to the Son, that all may honor the Son just as they honor the Father. He who does not honor the Son does not honor the Father, who sent him.

"I tell you the truth, whoever hears my word and believes him who sent me has eternal life and will not be condemned; he has crossed over from death to life. I tell you the truth, a time is coming and has now come when the dead will hear the voice of the Son of God and those who hear will live. For as the Father has life in himself, so he has granted the Son to have life in himself. And he has given him authority to judge because he is the Son of Man.

"Do no be amazed at this, for a time is coming when all who are in their graves will hear his voice and come out– those who have done good will rise to live, and those who have done evil will rise to be condemned. By myself I can do nothing, I judge only as I hear, and my judgment is just, for I seek not to please myself but him who sent me.

"If I testify about myself, my testimony is not valid. There is another who testifies in my favor, and I know that his testimony about me is valid.

"You have sent to John[3] and he has testified to the truth. Not that I accept human testimony; but I mention it that you may be saved. John was a lamp that burned and gave light, and you chose for a time to enjoy his light.

"I have testimony weightier than that of John. For the very work that the Father has given me to finish, and which I am doing, testifies that the Father has sent me. And the Father who sent me has himself testified concerning me. You have never heard his voice nor seen his form, nor does his word dwell in you, for you do not believe the one he sent. You diligently study the Scriptures because you think that by them you possess eternal life. These are the Scriptures that testify about me, yet you refuse to come to me to have life.

"I do not accept praise from men, but I know you. I know that you do not have the love of God in your hearts. I have come in my Father's name, and you do not accept me; but if someone else comes in his own name, you will accept him. How can you believe if you accept praise from one another, yet make no effort to obtain the praise that comes from the only God?

"But do not think I will accuse you before the Father. Your accuser is Moses, on whom your hopes are set. If you believed Moses, you would believe me, for he wrote about me. But since you do not believe what he wrote, how are you going to believe what I say?"

[*It was Jesus' practice to travel from Galilee to celebrate the Jewish festivals in Jerusalem. The following events could have occurred in any one of those travels*]

(Lk. 13:22)

Then Jesus went through the towns and villages, teaching as he made his way to Jerusalem.

(Lk. 10:38-42)

As Jesus and his disciples were on their way, he came to a village where a woman named Martha opened her home to him. She had a sister called Mary, who sat at the Lord's feet listening to what he said. But Martha was distracted by all the preparations that had to be made. She came to him and asked. "Lord, don't you care that my sister has left me to do the work by myself? Tell her to help me!"

"Martha, Martha," the Lord answered, "you are worried and upset about many things, but only one thing is needed. Mary has chosen what is better, and it will not be taken away from her."

(Lk. 14:25-35)

Large crowds were traveling with Jesus, and turning to them he said. "If anyone comes to me and does not hate his father and mother, his wife and children, his brothers and sisters – yes, even his own life – he cannot be my disciple. And any anyone who does not carry his cross and follow me cannot be my disciple.

"Suppose one of you wants to build a tower. Will he not first sit down and estimate the cost to see if he has enough money to complete it? For if he lays the foundation and is not able to finish it, everyone who sees it will ridicule him, saying, 'This fellow began to build and was not able to finish.'

"Or suppose a king is about to go to war against another king. Will he not first sit down and consider whether he is able with ten thousand men to oppose the one coming against him with twenty thousand? If he is not able, he will send a delegation while the other is still a long way off and will ask for terms of peace. In the same way, any of you who does not give up everything he has cannot be my disciple.

"Salt is good, but if it loses its saltiness, how can it be made salty again? It is fit neither for the soil nor for the manure pile; it is thrown out [4]."He who has ears to hear, let him hear."

(Lk. 15:1-32)

Now the tax collectors and "sinners' were all gathering around to hear him. But the Pharisees and the teachers of the law muttered, "This man welcomes sinners and eats with them."

Then Jesus told them this parable: "Suppose one of you has a hundred sheep[5] and loses one of them. Does he not leave the ninety-nine in the open country and go after the lost sheep until he finds it? And when he finds it, he joyfully puts it on his shoulders and goes home. Then he calls his friends and neighbors together and says, 'Rejoice with me; I have found my lost sheep.' I tell you that in the same way there will be more rejoicing in heaven over one sinner who repents than over ninety-nine righteous persons who do not need to repent.

"Or suppose a woman has ten silver coins and loses one. Does she not light a lamp, sweep the house and search carefully until she finds it? And when she finds it, she calls her friends and neighbors together and says, 'Rejoice with me; I have found my lost coin.' In the same way, I tell you, there is rejoicing in the presence of the angels of God over one sinner who repents."

Jesus continued: "There was a man who had two sons. The younger one said to his father, 'Father, give me my share of the estate.' So he divided his property between them.

"Not long after that, the younger son got together all he had, set off for a distant country and there squandered his wealth in wild living. After he had spent everything, there was a severe famine in that whole country, and he began to be in need. So he went and hired himself out to a citizen of that country, who sent him to his fields to feed pigs. He longed to fill his stomach with the pods that the pigs were eating, but no one gave him anything.

"When he came to his senses, he said, 'How many of my father's hired men have food to spare, and here I am starving to death! I will set out and go back to my father and say to him; Father, I have sinned against heaven and against you. I am no longer worthy to be called your son; make me like one of your hired men.' So he got up and went to his father.

"But while he was still a long way off, his father saw him and was filled with compassion for him; he ran to his son, threw his arms around him and kissed him.

"The son said to him, 'Father, I have sinned against heaven and against you. I am no longer worthy to be called your son.'

"But the father said to his servants, 'Quick! Bring the best robe and put it on him. Put a ring on his finger and sandals on his feet. Bring the fattened calf and kill it. Let's have a feast and celebrate. For this son of mine was dead and is alive again; he was lost and is found.' So they began to celebrate.

Meanwhile, the older son was in the field. When he came near the house, he heard music and dancing. So he called one of the servants and asked him what was going on. 'Your brother has come,' he replied, 'and your father has killed the fattened calf because he has him back safe and sound.'

'The older brother became angry and refused to go in. So his father went out and pleaded with him. But he answered his father, 'Look! All these years I've been slaving for you and never disobeyed your orders. Yet you never gave me even a young goat so I could celebrate with my friends. But when this son of yours who has squandered your property with prostitutes comes home, you kill the fattened calf for him!'

" 'My son,' the father said, 'you are always with me, and everything I have is yours. But we had to celebrate and be glad, because this brother of yours was dead and is alive again; he was lost and is found.'"

(Lk. 16:1-15)

Jesus told his disciples: 'there was a rich man whose manager was accused of wasting his possessions. So he called him in and asked him, 'what is this I hear about you? Give an account of your management, because you cannot be manager any longer.'

"The manager said to himself, 'what shall I do now? My master is taking away my job. I'm not strong enough to dig, and I'm ashamed to beg – I know what I'll do so that, when I lose my job here, people will welcome me into their houses.'

"So he called in each one of his master's debtors. He asked the first, 'How much do you owe my master?'

"'Eight hundred gallons of olive oil,' he replied.

"The manager told him, 'Take your bill, sit down quickly, and make it four hundred.'

"Then he asked the second, 'and how much do you owe?'

"'A thousand bushels of wheat,' he replied.

"He told him, 'Take your bill and make it eight hundred.'

"The master commended the dishonest manager because he had acted shrewd. For the people of this would are more shrewd in dealing with their own kind than are the people of the light. I tell you, use worldly wealth to gain friends for yourselves, so that when it is gone, you will be welcomed into eternal dwellings.

"Whoever can be trusted with very little can also be trusted with much, and whoever is dishonest with very little will also be dishonest with much. So if you have not been trustworthy in handling worldly wealth, who will trust you with true riches? And if you have not been trustworthy with someone else's property, who will give you property of your own?

"No servant can serve two masters. Either he will hate the one and love the other, or he will be devoted to the one and despise the other. You cannot serve both God andMoney[6]."

The Pharisees, who loved money, heard all this and were sneering at Jesus. He said to them, "You are the ones who justify yourselves in the eyes of men, but God knows your hearts. What is highly valued among men is detestable in God's sight.

(Lk. 16:19-31)

"There was a rich man who was dressed in purple and fine linen and lived in luxury every day. At his gate was laid a beggar named Lazarus, covered with sores and longing to eat what fell from the rich man's table. Even the dogs came and licked his sores.

"The time came when the beggar died and the angels carried him to Abraham's side. The rich man also died and was buried. In hell, where he was in torment, he looked up and saw Abraham far away, with Lazarus by his side. So he called to him, 'Father Abraham, have pity on me and send Lazarus to dip the tip of his finger in water and cool my tongue, because I am in agony in this fire.'

"But Abraham replied, 'Son remember that in your lifetime you received your good things, while Lazarus received bad things, but now he is comforted here and you are in agony. And besides all this, between us and you a great chasm has been fixed, so that those who want to go from here to you cannot, nor can anyone cross over from there to us.'

"He answered, 'Then I beg you, father, send Lazarus to my father's house, for I have five brothers. Let him warn them, so that they will not also come to this place to torment.'

"Abraham replied, 'They have Moses and the Prophets; let them listen to them.'

"'No, father Abraham, 'he said, 'but if someone from the dead goes to them, they will repent.'

"He said to him, 'If they do not listen to Moses and the Prophets, they will not be convinced even if someone rises from the dead.'"

(Lk. 17:11-21)

Now on his way to Jerusalem, Jesus traveled along the border between Samaria and Galilee. As he was going into a village, ten men who had leprosy met him. They stood at a distance and called out in a loud voice, "Jesus, Master, have pity on us!"

When he saw them, he said, "Go, show yourselves to the priests." And as they went, they were cleansed.

One of them, when he saw he was healed, came back, praising God in a loud voice. He threw himself at Jesus' feet and thanked him – and he was a Samaritan.

Jesus asked, "Were not all ten cleansed? Where are the other nine? Was no one found to return and give praise to God except this foreigner?" Then he said to him, "Rise and go; your faith has made you well."

Once, having been asked by the Pharisees when the kingdom of God would come, Jesus replied, "The kingdom of God does not come with your careful observation, nor will people say, 'Here it is,' or 'There it is,' because the kingdom of God is within you."

STUDY NOTES

1. Every year Jesus used to go to Jerusalem in March /April to celebrate the Passover festival as well as in September/ October for the Feast of Tabernacles.

2. He betrays the one who had done him a great miracle. By this he earns the dubious distinction of being the first betrayer- even ahead of Judas! We find one person who is just the opposite in Chapter 19 Study Note No:7.

3. Jesus refers to John four times during His ministry. This is the first time. The others are as follows:

    Second: Chapter 13 Study Note No.: 2

    Third: Chapter 18 Study Note No.: 3

    Fourth: Chapter 26 Study Note No.: 3

4. This is the first instance of Jesus telling the parable of salt-saltiness. He uses the same parable again twice. See Chapter 9 Study Note No.:3 and Chapter 2 Study Note No.: 12.

5. This is the first instance of Jesus telling the parable of hundred sheep which He uses it once more. See Chapter 18 Study Note No: 11.

6. Jesus gives this caution twice, once here and again in the Sermon on the Mount. See Chapter 9 study Note No.: 7

VIII

DIFFERENCE OF OPINION WITH THE RELIGIOUS LEADERS IN GALILEE

(Mt. 12:1-8 / Mk. 2:23-28 / Lk. 6:1-5)

One Sabbath[1] Jesus was going through the grain fields, and his disciples began to pick some heads of grain, rub them in their hands and eat the kernels. The Pharisees said to him, "Look, why are they doing what is unlawful on the Sabbath?"

He answered, "Haven't you read what David did when he and his companions were hungry in the days of Abiathar the high priest? He entered the house of God and ate the consecrated bread, which is lawful only for priests to eat. And he also gave some to his companions.

"Or haven't you read in the Law that on the Sabbath the priests in the temple desecrate the day and yet are innocent? I tell you that one greater than the temple is here. If you had known what these words mean, 'I desire mercy, not sacrifice,' you would not have condemned the innocent. The Sabbath was made for man, not man for the Sabbath. For the Son of Man is Lord of the Sabbath."

(Mt. 12:9-21 / Mk. 3:1-6 / Lk. 6:6-11)

On another Sabbath he went into the synagogue and was teaching, and a man was there whose right hand was shriveled. The Pharisees and the teachers of the law were looking for a reason to accuse Jesus, so they watched him closely to see if he would heal on the Sabbath and asked him, "Is it lawful to heal on the Sabbath?"

He said to them, "If any of you has a sheep and it falls into a pit on the Sabbath, will you not take hold of it and lift it out? How much more valuable is a man than a sheep! Therefore it is lawful to do good on the Sabbath."

But Jesus knew what they were thinking and said to the man with the shriveled hand, "Get up and stand in front of everyone." So he got up and stood there.

Then Jesus said to them "I ask you, which is lawful on the Sabbath: to do good or to do evil, to save life or to destroy it?" But they remained silent.

He looked around at them in anger and, deeply distressed at their stubborn hearts, said to the man, "Stretch out your hand." He stretched it out, and his hand was completely restored. But the Pharisees were furious. They went out and began to plot with the Herodians how they might kill Jesus.

Aware of this, Jesus withdrew from that place with his disciples to the lake. Many followed him, and he healed all their sick, warning them not to tell who he was. This was to fulfill what was spoken through the prophet Isaiah:

"Here is my servant whom I have chosen,
the one I love, in whom I delight;
I will put my Spirit on him,
and he will proclaim justice to the nations.
He will not quarrel or cry out;
no one will hear his voice in the streets,
A bruised reed he will not break;
and a smoldering wick he will not snuff out,
till he leads justice to victory.
In his name the nations will put their
hope."

(Lk. 13:10-17)

On a Sabbath Jesus was teaching in one of the synagogues, and a woman was there who had been crippled by a spirit for eighteen years. She was bent over and could not straighten up at all. When Jesus saw her, he called her forward and said to her, "Woman, you are set free from your infirmity." Then he put his hands on her, and immediately she straightened up and praised God.

Indignant because Jesus had healed on the Sabbath, the synagogue ruler said to the people, "There are six days for work. So come and be healed on those days, not on the Sabbath."

The Lord answered him, "You hypocrites! Doesn't each of you on the Sabbath untie his ox or donkey from the stall and lead it out to give it water? Then should not this woman, a daughter of Abraham, whom Satan has kept bound for eighteen long years, be set free on the Sabbath day from what bound her?"

When he said this, all his opponents were humiliated, but the people were delighted with all the wonderful things he was doing.

(Lk. 14:1-24)

One Sabbath, when Jesus went to eat in the house of a prominent Pharisee, he was being carefully watched. There in front of him was a man suffering from dropsy. Jesus asked the Pharisees and experts in the law, "Is it lawful to heal on the Sabbath or not?" But they remained silent. So taking hold of the man, he healed him and sent him away.

Then he asked them, "If one of you has a donkey or an ox that falls into a well on the Sabbath day, will you not immediately pull him out?" And they had nothing to say.

When he noticed how the guests picked the places of honor at the table, he told them this parable: "When someone invites you to a wedding feast, do not take the place of honor, for a person more distinguished than you may have been invited. If so, the host who invited both of you will come and say to you, 'Give this man your seat.' Then, humiliated, you will have to take the least important place. But when you are invited, take the lowest place, so that when your host comes, he will say to you, 'Friend, move up to a better place.' Then you will be honored in the presence of all your fellow guests. For everyone who exalts himself will be humbled, and he who humbles himself will be exalted."

Then Jesus said to his host, "When you give a luncheon or dinner, do not invite your friends, your brothers or relatives, or your rich neighbors; if you do, they may invite you back and so you will be repaid. But when you give a banquet, invite the poor, the crippled, the lame, the blind, and you will be blessed. Although they cannot repay you, you will be repaid at the resurrection of the righteous."

When one of those at the table with him heard this, he said to Jesus, "Blessed is the man who will eat at the feast in the kingdom of God."

Jesus replied: "A certain man was preparing a great banquet and invited many guests. At the time of the banquet he sent his servant to tell those who had been invited, 'come, for everything is now ready.'

"But they all alike began to make excuses. The first said, 'I have just bought a field, and I must go and see it, Please excuse me.'

"Another said, 'I have just bought five yoke of oxen, and I'm on my way to try them out. Please excuse me.'

"Still another said, 'I just got married, so I can't come.'

"The servant came back and reported this to his master. Then the owner of the house became angry and ordered his servant, 'Go out quickly into the streets and alleys of the town and bring in the poor, the crippled, the blind and the lame.'

"'Sir', the servant said, 'what you ordered has been done, but there is still room.'

"Then the master told his servant, 'Go out to the roads and country lanes and make them come in, so that my house will be full. I tell you, not one of those men who were invited will get a taste of my banquet.'"

STUDY NOTES

1. This is the Sabbath day which comes in the second day after the Passover. That means that almost six months had past since Jesus returned from Jerusalem after the Feast of Tabernacles. There is no record of the events that occurred during this six months period in all the four gospels. And the fact that He is back in Galilee just within two days of the festival is notable. This is the second Passover feast Jesus celebrates during His ministry. For the other Passover Feasts refer the following:

I Passover: Chapter 5 Study Note No. 1

III Passover: Chapter 16 Study Note No.3

IV Passover: Chapter 22 Study Note No. 2

IX
SERMON ON THE MOUNT

(Mk. 3:7-19 / Lk. 6:12-19)

One of those days, Jesus went out to a mountainside [*near the lake*] to pray, and spent the night praying to God. When morning came, he called his disciples to him and chose twelve of them, whom he also designated apostles[1] that they might be with him and that he might send them out to preach and to have authority to drive out demons: There were the twelve he appointed:

1. **Simon** (whom he named Peter)

2. his brother **Andrew**

3. **James**

4. **John** (to them he gave them the name Boanerges,which means Sons of Thunder)

5. **Philip**

6. **Bartholomew**

7. **Matthew**

8. **Thomas**

9. **James** son of Alphaeus

10. **Simon** who was called the Zealot

11. **Judas** son of James, [*Thaddaeus?*] and

12. **Judas Iscariot**, who became a traitor.

He went down with them and stood on a level place. A large crowd of his disciples was there and a great number of people from all over Judea, from Galilee, Jerusalem, and from the coast of Tyre and Sidon, Idumea and the regions across the Jordan, who had come to hear him and to be healed of their diseases. Those troubled by evil spirits were cured.

And the people all tried to touch him, because power was coming from him and healing them all. Whenever the evil spirits saw him, they fell down before him and cried out, "You are the Son of God." But he gave them strict orders not to tell who he was.

Because of the crowd he told his disciples to have a small boat ready for him, to keep the people from crowding him.

(Mt. 5:1-7:29 / Lk. 6:20-44,46-7:1, 11:1-13,33-36, 12:13-34,57-59, 13:1-9, 23-27 & 16:17)

When he sat down, his disciples came to him, and he began to teach them, saying [2]: "Blessed are the poor in spirit,
for theirs is the kingdom of heaven.
Blessed are those who mourn,
for they will be comforted.
Blessed are the meek,
for they will inherit the earth.
Blessed are those who hunger and thirst for
righteousness,
for they will be filled.
Blessed are the merciful,
for they will be shown mercy.
Blessed are the pure in heart,
for they will see God.
Blessed are the peacemakers,
for they will be called sons of God.
Blessed are those who are persecuted because
of righteousness,
for theirs is the kingdom of heaven.
Blessed are you who are poor,
for yours is the kingdom of God.
Blessed are you who hunger now,
for you will be satisfied.
Blessed are you who weep now,
for you will laugh,
"Blessed are you when people hate you, when they exclude you, insult you, persecute you and falsely say all kinds of evil against you because of me. Rejoice in that day and leap for joy, because great is your reward in heaven for in the same way they persecuted the prophets who were before you.

"But woe to you who are rich,

for you have already received your comfort.
Woe to you who are well fed now,
for you will go hungry.
Woe to you who laugh now,
for you will mourn and weep.
Woe to you when all men speak well of you,
for that is how their fathers treated the false prophets.

"You are the salt of the earth[3]. But if the salt loses its saltiness, how can it be made salty again? It is no longer good for anything, except to be thrown out and trampled by men.

"You are the light of the world. A city on a hill cannot be hidden. Neither do people light a lamp and put it in a place where it will be hidden or under a bowl. Instead they put it on its stand, so that those who come in may see the light and it gives light to everyone in the house. In the same way, let your light shine before men, that they may see your good deeds and praise your Father in heaven.

"Do not think that I have come to abolish the Law or the Prophets; I have not come to abolish them but to fulfill them. I tell you the truth, until heaven and earth disappear, not the smallest letter, not the least stroke of a pen, will by any means disappear from the Law until everything is accomplished. It is easier for the heaven and earth to disappear than for the least stroke of the pen to drop out of the Law. Anyone who breaks one of the least of these commandments and teaches others to do the same will be called least in the kingdom of heaven, but whoever practices and teaches these commands will be called great in the kingdom of heaven.

"For I tell you that unless your righteousness surpasses that of the Pharisees and the teachers of the law, you will certainly not enter the kingdom of heaven.

"You have heard that it was said to the people long ago, 'Do not murder, and anyone who murders will be subject to judgment.' But I tell you that anyone who is angry with his brother without cause will be subject to judgment. Again, anyone who says to his brother, 'Raca,' is answerable to the Sanhedrin. But anyone who says, 'You fool!' will be in danger of the fire of hell.

"Therefore, if you are offering your gift at the altar and there remember that your brother has something against you[4], leave your gift there in front of the altar. First go and be reconciled to your brother; then come and offer your gift.

"Why don't you judge for yourselves what is right ?[5] Settle matters quickly with your adversary who is taking you to court. Do it while you are still with him on the way, or he may hand you over to the judge, and the judge may hand you over to the officer, and you may be thrown into prison. I tell you the truth, you will not get out until you have paid the last penny."

Now there were some present at that time who told Jesus about the Galileans whose blood Pilate had mixed with their sacrifices. Jesus answered, "Do you think that these Galileans were worse sinners than all the other Galileans because they suffered this way? I tell you, no! But unless you repent, you too will all perish. Or those eighteen who died when the tower in Siloam fell on them –do you think they were more guilty than all the others living in Jerusalem? I tell you, no! but unless you repent, you too will all perish."

Then he told this parable: "A man had a fig tree, planted in this vineyard, and he went to look for fruit on it, but did not find any. So he said to the man who took care of the vineyard, 'For three years now I've been coming to look for fruit on this fig tree and haven't found any. Cut it down! Why should it use up the soil?'

" 'Sir,' the man replied, 'leave it alone for one more year, and I'll dig around it and fertilize it. If it bears fruit next year, fine! If not, then cut it down.'

"You have heard that it was said, 'Do not commit adultery.' But I tell you that anyone who looks at a woman lustfully has already committed adultery with her in his heart. If your right eye causes you to sin, gouge it out and throw it away. It is better for you to lose one part of your body than for your whole body to be thrown into hell. And if your right hand causes you to sin, cut it off and throw it away. It is better for you to lose one part of your body than for your whole body to go into hell.

"It had been said, 'Anyone who divorces his wife must give her a certificate of divorce.' But I tell you that anyone who divorces his wife, except for martial unfaithfulness, causes her to become an adulteress, and anyone who marries the divorced woman commits adultery.

"Again, you have heard that it was said to the people long ago, 'Do not break your oath, but keep the oaths you have made to the Lord.' But I tell you, Do not swear at all: either by heaven, for it is God's throne; or by the earth, for it is his foot-stool; or by Jerusalem, for it is the city of the Great King. And do not swear by your head, for you cannot make even one hair white or black. Simply let your 'Yes' be 'Yes', and your 'No,' 'No'; anything beyond this comes from the evil one.

"You have heard that it was said, 'Eye for eye, and tooth for tooth.' But I tell you, Do not resist an evil person. If someone strikes you on the right cheek, turn to him the other also. And if someone wants to sue you and take your tunic, let him have your cloak as well. If someone forces you to go one mile, go with him two miles. Give to the one who asks you, and do not turn away from the one who wants to borrow from you. And if anyone takes what belongs to you, do not demand it back. do to others as you would have them do to you.

"You have heard that it was said, 'Love your neighbor and hate your enemy.' But I tell you who hear me: Love your enemies do good to those who hate you, bless those who curse you and pray for those who persecute you, that you may be sons of your Father the most high in heaven. He causes his sun to rise on the evil and the good, and sends rain on the righteous and the unrighteous. If you love those who love you, what reward will you get? Are not even the tax collectors doing that? And if you greet only your brothers, what are you doing more than others? Do not even pagans do that? And if you do good to those who are good to you, what credit is that to you? Even 'sinners' do that. And if you lend to those from whom you expect repayment, what credit is that to you? Even 'sinners' lend to 'sinners,' expecting to be repaid in full. But love your enemies, do good to them, and lend to them without expecting to get anything back. Then your reward will be great, and you will be sons of the Most High, because he is kind to the ungrateful and wicked. Be merciful, just as your Father is merciful. Be perfect, therefore, as your heavenly Father is perfect.

"Be careful not to do your 'acts of righteousness' before men, to be seen by them. If you do, you will have no reward from your Father in heaven.

"So when you give to the needy, do not announce it with trumpets, as the hypocrites do in the synagogues and on the street, to be honored by men. I tell you the truth, they have received their reward in full. But when you give to the needy, do not let your left hand know what your right hand is doing, so that your giving may be in secret. Then your Father, who sees what is done in secret, will reward you.

"And when you pray, do not be like the hypocrites, for they love to pray standing in the synagogues and on the street corners to be seen by men. I tell you the truth, they have received their reward in full. But when you pray, go into your room, close the door and pray to your Father, who is unseen. Then your Father, who sees what is done in secret, will reward you. And when you pray, do not keep on babbling like pagans, for they think they will be heard because of their many words. Do not be like them, for your Father knows what you need before you ask him."

[6] One of his disciples said to him, "Lord, teach us to pray, just as John taught his disciples."

He said to them, "This, then, is how you should pray:

" 'Our Father in heaven,
hallowed be your name,
your kingdom come,
your will be done
on earth as it is in heaven.
Give us today our daily bread.
Forgive us our debts,
as we also have forgiven our debtors.
And lead us not into temptation,
but deliver us from the evil
For yours is the kingdom
and power and glory forever. Amen.'

"For if you forgive men when they sin against you, your heavenly Father will also forgive you. But if you do not forgive men their sins, your Father will not forgive your sins.

"When you fast, do not look somber as the hypocrites do, for they disfigure their faces to show men they are fasting. I tell you the truth, they have received their reward in full. But when you fast, put oil on your head and wash your face, so that it will not be obvious to men that you are fasting, but only to your Father, who is unseen; and your Father, who sees what is done in secret, will reward you.

Someone in the crowd said to him, "Teacher, tell my brother to divide the inheritance with me."

Jesus replied, "Man, who appointed me a judge or an arbiter between you?" Then he said to them, "Watch out! Be on your guard against all kinds of greed; a man's life does not consist in the abundance of his possessions."

And he told them this parable: "The ground of a certain rich man produced a good crop. He thought to himself, 'What shall I do? I have no place to store my crops.'

"Then he said, 'This is what I'll do. I will tear down my barns and build bigger ones, and there I will store all my grain and my goods. And I'll say to myself, "You have plenty of good things laid up for many years. Take life easy; eat, drink and be merry."'

"But God said to him, 'You fool! This very night your life will be demanded from you. Then who will get what you have prepared for yourself?'

"This is how it will be with anyone who stores up things for himself but is not rich toward God."

Then Jesus said to his disciples: "Therefore I tell you, do not worry about your life, what you will eat or drink; or about your body, what you will wear. Life is more than food, and the body more than clothes. Consider the ravens: They do not sow or reap, they have no storeroom or barn; yet God feeds them. And how much more valuable you are than birds! Who of you by worrying can add a single cubit to his height? Since you cannot do this very little thing, why do you worry about the rest?

"And why do you worry about clothes? Consider how the lilies grow. They do not labor or spin. Yet I tell you, not even Solomon in all his splendor was dressed like one of these. If that is how God clothes the grass of the field, which is here today, and tomorrow is thrown into the fire, how much more will he clothe you, O you of little faith! And do not set your heart on what you will eat or drink or wear? Do not worry about it. For the pagan world runs after all such things, and your heavenly Father knows that you need them. But seek first his kingdom and his righteousness, and all these things will be given to you as well. Therefore do not worry about tomorrow, for tomorrow will worry about itself. Each day has enough trouble of its own.

"Do not be afraid, little flock, for your Father has been pleased to give you the kingdom. Sell your possessions and give to the poor. Provide purses for yourselves that will not wear out a treasure in heaven that will not be exhausted. Do not store up for yourselves treasures on earth, where moth and rust destroy, and where thieves break in and steal. But store up for yourselves treasures in heaven, where moth and rust do not destroy, and where thieves do not break in and steal. For where your treasure is, there your heart will be also.

"The eye is the lamp of the body. If your eyes are good, your whole body will be full of light. But if your eyes are bad, your whole body will be full of darkness. If then the light within you is darkness, how great is that darkness! See to it, then, that the light within you is not darkness. Therefore, if your whole body is full of light, and not part of it dark, it will be completely lighted, as when the light of a lamp shines on you.

"No one can serve two masters. Either he will hate the one and love the other, or he will be devoted to the one and despise the other. You cannot serve both God and Money.[7]

"Do not judge, and you will not be judged. Do not condemn, and you will not be condemned. For in the same way you judge others, you will be judged.

"Forgive, and you will be forgiven. Give, and it will be given to you. A good measure, pressed down, shaken together and running over, will be poured into your lap. For with the measure you use, it will be measured to you."

He also told them this parable: "Can a blind man lead a blind man? Will they not both fall into a pit? A student is not above his teacher, but everyone who is fully trained will be like his teacher.

"Why do you look at the speck of sawdust in your brother's eye and pay no attention to the plank in your own eye? How can you say to your brother, 'Brother, let me take the speck out of your eye,' when you yourself fail to see the plank in your own eye? You hypocrite, first take the plank out of your eye, and then you will see clearly to remove the speck from your brother's eye.

"Do not give dogs what is sacred; do not throw your pearls to pigs. If you do, they may trample them under their feet, and then turn and tear you to pieces."

Then he said to them, "Suppose one of you has a friend, and he goes to him at midnight and says, 'Friend, lend me three loaves of bread, because a friend of mine on a journey has come to me, and I have nothing to set before him.'

"Then the one inside answers, 'Don't bother me. The door is already locked, and my children are with me in bed. I can't get up and give you anything.' I tell you, though he will not get up and give him the bread because he is his friend, yet because of the man's boldness he will get up and give him as much as he needs.

"So I say to you: Ask and it will be given to you; seek and you will find; knock and the door will be opened to you. For everyone who asks receives; he who seeks finds; and to him who knocks, the door will be opened.

"Which of you fathers, if your son asks for bread, will give him a stone? Or if he asks for a fish, will give him a snake instead? Or if he asks for an egg, will give him a scorpion? If you then, though you are evil, know how to give good gifts to your children, how much more will your Father in heaven give the Holy Spirit to those who ask him!

"So in everything, do to others what you would have them do to you, for this sums up the Law and the Prophets."

Someone asked him, "Lord, are only a few people going to be saved?"

He said to them, "Make every effort to enter through the narrow door, because many, I tell you, will try to enter and will not be able to.

"For wide is the gate and broad is the road that leads to destruction, and many enter through it. But small is the gate and narrow the road that leads to life, and only a few find it.

"Watch out for false prophets. They come to you in sheep's clothing, but inwardly they are ferocious wolves. By their fruit you will recognize them. Do people pick grapes from thorn-bushes, or figs from thistles? Likewise every good tree bears good fruit, but a bad tree bears bad fruit. A good tree cannot bear bad fruit, and a bad tree cannot bear good fruit. Every tree that does not bear good fruit is cut down and thrown into the fire. Thus, by their fruit you will recognize them.

"Not everyone who says to me, 'Lord, Lord,' will enter the kingdom of heaven, but only he who does the will of my Father who is in heaven. Many will say to me on that day, 'Lord, Lord, did we not prophesy in your name, and in your name drive out demons and perform many miracles?' Then I will tell them plainly, 'I never knew you. Away from me, you evildoers!'

Once the owner of the house gets up and closes the door, you will stand outside knocking and pleading, 'Sir, open the door for us.'

"But he will answer, 'I don't know you or where you come from.'

"Then you will say, 'We ate and drank with you, and you taught in our streets.'

"But he will reply, 'I don't know you or where you come from. Away from me, all you evildoers!'

"Why do you call me, 'Lord, Lord,' and do not do what I say? Therefore I will show you what everyone who hears these words of mine and puts them into practice is like. He is like a man building a house, who dug down deep and laid the foundation on rock. The rain came down, the streams rose, and the winds blew and beat against that house but could not shake it. It did not fall. Because it was well built. But everyone who hears these words of mine and does not put them into practice is like a foolish man who built his house on sand without a foundation. The rain came down, the streams rose, and the winds blew and beat against that house, and it fell with a great crash."

When Jesus had finished saying all this in the hearing of the people the crowds were amazed at his teaching, because he taught as one who had authority, and not as their teachers of the law.

STUDY NOTES

1. There are two lists of names given in the gospels. This one is the list of twelve apostles chosen from among the disciples. See Chapter 15 Study Note No.:1 for the other list.

2. This is the Sermon that Jesus gave on the mount. Although Mathew gives this Sermon in one stretch from Mt. 5:1 – 8:1, Luke gives it in nine different parts of his Gospel. There is a school of thought that it was not a one-stretch Sermon but Mathew had assembled many Sermons into one. After considering the whole portion in totality I can't but subscribe to the view that it was a <u>one-stretch Sermon only.</u> The following are the reasons that led to that conclusion:

a) It is to be noted that the Sermon which begins in Mt. 5:3 goes nonstop up to Mt. 7:27.

b) When seen in the angle that this was the first instructions given to the twelve apostles chosen after a nightlong prayer, every part of this Sermon fits in well.

c) Moreover in Luke's Gospel where the same content is given in nine different places, it is obvious they do not fit into that context but to the one stated above. For example we see in Lk.12:1 he starts by saying "... when a crowd of many thousands..." this is not possible in that context because the said place is a Pharisee's house (Lk. 11:37). Here in Lk. 12:13-34 we see a portion of the Sermon on the mount. Therefore it is more possible that it is indeed a part of Sermon on the mount than inside a Pharisee's house. As we see in Study Note No.5, Luke has not given as much importance Mathew has given to the chronological sequence. By this, we can conclude that this Sermon was indeed a <u>one-stretch Sermon only.</u>

3. This is the second of the three times Jesus uses the parable 'salt –

saltiness'. For the other two, refer to Chapter 7 Study Note No.: 4 & Chapter 18 Study Note No.:12.

4. For instruction on 'when you have something against your brother...' see Chapter 25 Study Note No.: 2.

5. Luke's style of presentation of the Gospel is saying 'whatever that happened' and not saying it as 'as they happened'. In Mathew and Mark the Gospel story is told in the latter manner giving more importance to the chronological sequence than Luke.

Moreover, in the Gospel of Luke, we find the words like 'one day', 'while', mentioned quite often. These expressions more often than not suggest that the following incident is not given in chronological order. There are nearly forty-four such occurrences in his Gospel. It is thus necessary that every incident given in the Gospel of Luke has to be viewed in the light of other three Gospels to find out "WHAT HAPPENED - WHEN".

6. Luke must be referring to the nightlong prayer that Jesus had prayed before this Sermon. (Lk. 11:1)

7. The same was taught earlier. Chapter 25 Study Note No.: 6.

X
MINISTRY WITH THE APOSTLES

(Mt. 8:1-4 /Mk. 1:40-45 / LK. 5:12-16)

When he came down from the mountain side, large crowds followed him. A man with leprosy came and when he saw Jesus, he fell with his face to the ground and knelt before him and said, "Lord, if you are willing, you can make me clean."

Jesus reached out his hand and touched the man. "I am willing," he said. "Be clean!" Immediately he was cured of his leprosy. Then Jesus said to him, "See that you don't tell anyone. But go, show yourself to the priest and offer the gift Moses commanded, as a testimony to them."

Instead he went out and began to talk freely, spreading the news. As a result, Jesus could no longer enter a town openly but stayed outside in lonely places. Yet the people still came to him from everywhere to hear him and to be healed of their sickness. But Jesus often withdrew to lonely places and prayed.

(Mt. 8:5-13 / Lk. 7:1-10 & 13:28-30)

When Jesus had entered Capernaum, there a centurion's servant, whom his master valued highly, was sick [*Paralyzed*] and about to die. The centurion heard of Jesus and sent some elders of the Jews [*the ones that wanted to kill him!*] to him, asking him to come and heal his servant. When they came to Jesus, they pleaded earnestly with him, "This man deserves to have you do this, because he loves our nation and has built our synagogue." So Jesus went with them.

He was not far from the house when the centurion sent friends to say to him: "Lord, don't trouble yourself, for I do not deserve to have you come under my roof. That is why I did not even consider myself worthy to come to you. But say a word, and my servant will be healed. For I myself am a man under authority, with soldiers under me. I tell this one, 'Go,' and he goes; and that one, 'Come,' and he comes. I say to my servant, 'Do this,' and he does it."

When Jesus heard this, he was amazed at him, and turning to the crowd following him, he said, "I tell you the truth, I have not found such great faith even in Israel. There will be weeping there, and gnashing of teeth, when you see Abraham, Isaac and Jacob and all the prophets in the kingdom of God, but you yourselves thrown out. People will come from east and west and north and south, and will take their places at the feast in the kingdom of God. Indeed there are those who are last who will be first, and first who will be last."

Then Jesus said to the centurion [1] [*to his messengers*], "Go! It will be done just as you believed it would." And his servant was healed at that very hour. Then the men who had been sent returned to the house and found the servant well.

(Lk. 7:11-17)

Soon afterward, Jesus went to a town called Nain, and his disciples and a large crowd went along with him. As he approached the town gate, a dead person was being carried out – the only son of his mother, and she was a widow. And a large crowd from the town was with her. When the Lord saw her, his heart went out to her and he said, "Don't cry."

Then he went up and touched the coffin, and those carrying it stood still. He said, "Young man, I say to you, get up!" The dead man sat up and began to talk, and Jesus gave him back to his mother.

They were all filled with awe and praised God. "A great prophet has appeared among us," they said. "God has come to help his people." This news about Jesus spread throughout Judea[2] and the surrounding country

(Mt. 12:22-37 / Mk. 3:20,22-30 / Lk. 6:45, 11:14,15,17-23,12:10)

Then Jesus entered a house[3] , and again a crowd gathered, so that he and his disciples were not even able to eat.

Then they brought him a demon-possessed man who was blind and mute, and Jesus healed him, so that he could both talk and see. All the people were astonished and said, "Could this be the 'Son of David?'"

But when the Pharisees and the teachers of the law who came down from Jerusalem [4] heard this, they said, "It is only by Beelzebub, the prince of demons, that this fellow drives out demons.[5]"

Jesus knew their thoughts. He called them and spoke to them in parables: "How can Satan drive out Satan? If a kingdom is divided against itself, that kingdom cannot stand." "Every kingdom divided against itself will be ruined, and every city or household divided against itself will not stand. If Satan drives out Satan, he is divided against himself. How then can his kingdom stand? And if I drive out demons by Beelzebub, by whom do your people drive them out? So then, they will be your judges. But if I drive out demons by the Spirit of God, then the kingdom of God has come upon you. When a strong man, fully armed, guards his own house, his possessions are safe.

"Or again, how can anyone enter a strong man's house and carry off his possessions unless he first ties up the strong man? But when someone stronger attacks and overpowers him he takes away the armor in which the man trusted, rob his house and divide up the spoils.

"He who is not with me is against me, and he who does not gather with me scatters. And so I tell you, every sin and blasphemy will be forgiven men, but the blasphemy against the Spirit will not be forgiven. Anyone who speaks a word against the Son of Man will be forgiven, but anyone who speaks against the Holy Spirit will not be forgiven, either in this age or in the age to come. He is guilty of an eternal sin.

"Make a tree good and its fruit will be good, or make a tree bad and its fruit will be bad, for a tree is recognized by its fruit. You brood of vipers, how can you who are evil say anything good? For out of the overflow of the heart the mouth speaks. The good man brings good things out of the good stored up in him, and the evil man brings evil things out of the evil stored up in him. But I tell you that men will have to give account on the day of judgment for every careless word they have spoken. For by your words you will be acquitted, and by your words you will be condemned." He said this because they were saying, "He has an evil Spirit."

(Mt. 12:38-45/Lk. 11:16, 24-26, 29-32)
Then some of the Pharisees and teachers of the law tested him by asking, "Teacher, we want to see a miraculous sign from heaven.[6]"

He answered, "A wicked and adulterous generation asks for a miraculous sign! But none will be given it except the sign of the prophet Jonah. For as Jonah was three days and three nights in the belly of a huge fish, so the Son of Man will be three days and three nights in the heart of the earth. For as Jonah was a sign to the Ninevites, so also will the Son of Man be to this generation. The men of Nineveh will stand up at the judgment with this generation and condemn it; for they repented at the preaching of Jonah, and now one greater than Jonah is here. The Queen of the South will rise at the judgment with this generation and condemn it; for she came from the ends of the earth to listen to Solomon's wisdom, and now one greater than Solomon is here.

"When an evil spirit comes out of a man, it goes through arid places seeking rest and does not find it. Then it says, 'I will return to the house I left.' When it arrives, it finds the house unoccupied, swept clean and put in order. Then it goes and takes with it seven other spirits more wicked than itself, and they go in and live there. And the final condition of that man is worse than the first. That is how it will be with this wicked generation."

(Lk. 11:27,28)

As Jesus was saying these things, a woman in the crowd called out, "Blessed is the mother who gave you birth and nursed you."

He replied, "Blessed rather are those who hear the word of God and obey it."

(Mt. 12:46-50 / Mk. 3:21,31-35 / Lk. 8:19-21)

When his family heard about this [*His return from the wilderness*] , they went to take charge of him, for they said, "He is out of his mind." While Jesus was still talking to the crowd, his mother and brothers stood outside, wanting to speak to him, they sent someone in to call him.

Someone told him, "Your mother and brothers are standing outside, wanting to see you."

"Who are my mother and my brothers?" he asked. Then he looked at those seated in a circle around him and said pointing to his disciples, "Here are my mother and my brothers! For whoever does the will of my Father in heaven is my brother and sister and mother."

(Lk. 11:37-41)

When Jesus had finished speaking, a Pharisee[7] invited him to eat with him; so he went in and reclined at the table. But the Pharisee, noticing that Jesus did not first wash before the meal, was surprised.

Then the Lord said to him, "Now then, you Pharisees clean the outside of the cup and dish, but inside you are full of greed and wickedness. You foolish people! Did not the one who made the outside make the inside also? But give what is inside the dish to the poor, and everything will be clean for you." [8]

STUDY NOTES

1. Luke who gives a detailed account of this incident tells us that it was the messengers of the centurion who met Jesus. Mathew while giving a brief account of the same incident, says that the centurion met Jesus- meaning his messengers.

2. When it is stated that the news about this incident, which occurred in Galilee spread throughout the distant Judea, the extent to which it would have spread in Galilee itself can be well imagined!

3. Because of the popularity gained via the miracle in the town called Nain and by the publicity given by the cleansed leper, Jesus was unable to stay with in the town. Therefore He was staying in the wilderness outside the town for a few days. This incident happens on His return to the house after those few days.

4. The congregation of Pharisees and the teachers of the law from Jerusalem meeting Jesus on the day of His return is similar to the earlier occurrence, and is one among the three enquiry missions. See Chapter 6 Study Note No.: 1 & Chapter 17 Study Note No.: 3

5. This is the first time that the Pharisees are passing such a comment. Since being the first time, Jesus responds with a detailed reply. See Chapter 13 Study Note No.:1

6. They are asking for a proof of authority for His ministry and not just another miracle. This is the first time such a demand is made. Since this is the first time Jesus gives a detailed reply. The second time such a demand is made is in Chapter 17 Study Note No.:4.

7. This is a local Pharisee, who most probably was with those who had come from Jerusalem to interview Him. On going there Jesus does some tough talking.

8. The portion that follows this in Luke's Gospel (11:42 onwards) is actually a part of what He said in the temple - much later in His ministry.

XI

A SERMON OF PARABLES

(Mt. 13:1-9/ Mk. 4:1-9/ Lk. 8:4-8)

That same day Jesus went out of the house and sat by the lake and began to teach. Such large crowds gathered around him that he got into a boat and sat in it, while all the people stood on the shore. Then he told them many things in parables, saying:

Parable I

"A farmer went out to sow his seed. As he was scattering the seed, some fell along the path; it was trampled on, and the birds came and ate it up. Some fell on rocky places, where it did not have much soil. It sprang up quickly, because the soil was shallow. But when the sun came up, the plants were scorched, and they withered because they had no root and moisture. Other seed fell among thorns, which grew up with it so that it did not bear grain and choked the plants.

Still other seed fell on good soil. It came up, grew and produced a crop, multiplying thirty, sixty, or even a hundred times."

Then Jesus called out, "He who has ears to hear, let him hear."

Parable II

(Mt. 13:24-30)

Jesus told them another parable: "The kingdom of heaven is like a man who sowed good seed in his field. But while everyone was sleeping, his enemy came and sowed weeds among the wheat, and went away. When the wheat sprouted and formed heads, then the weeds also appeared.

"The owner's servants came to him and said, 'Sir, didn't you sow good seed in your field? Where then did the weeds come from?'

"'An enemy did this,' he replied.

"The servants asked him, 'Do you want us to go and pull them up?'

"'No,' he answered, 'because while you are pulling the weeds, you may root up the wheat with them. Let both grow together until the harvest. At that time I will tell the harvesters: First collect the weeds and tie them in bundles to be burned; then gather the wheat and bring it into my barn.'"

Parable III

(Mk. 4:26-29)

He also said, "This is what the kingdom of God is like. A man scatters seed on the ground. Night and day, whether he sleeps or gets up, the seed sprouts and grows, though he does not know how. All by itself the soil produces grain– first the stalk, then the head, then the full kernel in the head. As soon as the grain is ripe, he puts the sickle to it, because the harvest has come."

Parable IV

(Mt. 13:31,32 / Mk. 4:30-32 / Lk. 13:18,19)

Again he said, "What shall we say the kingdom of God is like, or what parable shall we use to describe it? The kingdom of heaven is like a mustard seed, which a man took and planted in his field. Though it is smallest of all your seeds you plant in the ground, yet when it grows, it is the largest of garden plants and becomes a tree, so that the birds of the air come and perch in its branches."

Parable V

(Mt. 13:33 / Lk. 13:20,21)

He told them still another parable: "The kingdom of heaven is like yeast that a woman took and mixed into a large amount of flour until it worked all through the dough."

(Mt. 13:34,35 / Mk. 4:33,34)

Jesus spoke all these things to the crowd in parables; With many similar parables Jesus spoke the word to them, as much as they could understand. He did not say anything to them without using a parable.

So was fulfilled what was spoken through the prophet: "I will open my mouth in parables, I will utter things hidden since the creation of the world."

But when he was alone with his own disciples, he explained everything.

(Mt. 13:10-23, 36 / Mk. 4:10-25 / Lk. 8:9-18)

Then he left the crowd and went into the house. When he was alone, the Twelve and the others around him asked him about the parables [*The sower and the seed*]. The disciples came to him and asked, "Why do you speak to the people in parables?"

He replied, "The knowledge of the secrets of the kingdom of heaven has been given to you, but not to them. Whoever has will be given more, and he will have an abundance. Whoever does not have, even what he has will be taken from him. This is why I speak to them in parables.

"Though seeing, they do not see;
though hearing, they do not hear or
understand; otherwise they might turn and be forgiven!
In them is fulfilled the prophecy of Isaiah:
"' You will be ever hearing but never
understanding;
you will be ever seeing but never perceiving.
For this people's heart has become calloused;
they hardly hear with their ears,
and they have closed their eyes.
Otherwise they might see with their eyes,
hear with their ears,
understand with their hearts
and turn,
and I would heal them.'
But blessed are your eyes because they see, and your ears because they hear. For I tell you the truth, many prophets and righteous men longed to see what you see but did not see it, and to hear what you hear but did not hear it."

Then Jesus said to them, "Don't you understand this parable? How then will you understand any parable? Listen then to what the parable of the sower means: The seed is 'the word of God'. The farmer sows 'the word'. When anyone hears the message about the kingdom and does not understand it, the devil comes and take away the word from their hearts, so that they may not believe and be saved. This is the seed sown along the path.

"Others, like seed sown on rocky places, hear the word and at once receive it with joy. But since he has no root, he believes for a while and lasts only a short time. When trouble or persecution comes because of the word, he quickly falls away.

"The seed that fell among thorns stands for those who hear, but the worries of this life, the deceitfulness of wealth and the desires for other things [*pleasures*] come in and choke the word, making it unfruitful.

"But the one who received the seed that fell on good soil is the man with a noble and good heart who hears the word, understands it and retains it. And by persevering produce a crop hundred, sixty or thirty times what was sown. No one lights a lamp and hides it in a jar or puts it under a bed. Instead, he puts it on a stand, so that those who come in can see the light. For there is nothing hidden that will not be disclosed, and nothing concealed that will not be known or brought out into the open. If anyone has ears to hear, let him hear."

"Therefore consider carefully how you listen. If anyone has ears to hear, let him hear. Consider carefully what you hear," he continued. "With the measure you use, it will be measured to you – even more. Whoever has will be given more; whoever does not have even what he thinks he has will be taken from him."

(Mt. 13:36-52)

His disciples came to him and said, "Explain to us the parable of the weeds in the field."

He answered, " 'The one who sowed the good seed' is the Son of Man. 'The field' is the world, and 'the good seed' stands for the sons of the kingdom. 'The weeds' are the sons of the evil one, and 'the enemy who sows' them is the devil. 'The harvest' is the end of the age, and 'the harvesters' are angels.

"As the weeds are pulled up and burned in the fire, so it will be at the end of the age. The Son of Man will send out his angels, and they will weed out of his kingdom everything that causes sin and all who do evil. They will throw them into the fiery furnace, where there will be weeping and gnashing of teeth. Then the righteous will shine like the sun in the kingdom of their Father. He who has ears, let him hear.

"The kingdom of heaven is like treasure hidden in a field. When a man found it, he hid it again, and then in his joy went and sold all he had and bought that field.

"Again, the kingdom of heaven is like a merchant looking for fine pearls. When he found one of great value, he went away and sold everything he had and bought it.

"Once again, the kingdom of heaven is like a net that was let down into the lake and caught all kinds of fish. When it was full, the fishermen pulled it up on the shore. Then they sat down and collected the good fish in baskets, but threw the bad away. This is how it will be at the end of the age. The angels will come and separate the wicked from the righteous and throw them into the fiery furnace, where there will be weeping and gnashing of teeth.

"Have you understood all these things?" Jesus asked.

"Yes," they replied.

He said to them, "Therefore every teacher of the law who has been instructed about the kingdom of heaven is like the owner of a house who brings out of his storeroom new treasures as well as old."

XII

THE WIND, THE WAVES AND THE LEGION

(Mt. 8: 18-27 / Mk. 4:35-41 / Lk. 8:22-25, 9: 57-62)

That day when evening came Jesus saw the crowd around him, he gave orders to cross to the other side of the lake. Then a teacher of the law came to him and said, "Teacher, I will follow you wherever you go."

Jesus replied, "Foxes have holes and birds of the air have nests, but the Son of Man has no place to lay his head."

He said to another disciple, "Follow me." But the man replied, "Lord, first let me go and bury my father."

Jesus said to him, "Let the dead bury their own dead, but you go and proclaim the kingdom of God."

Still another said, "I will follow you, Lord; but first let me go back and say good-bye to my family,"

Jesus replied, "No one who puts his hand to the plow and looks back is fit for service in the kingdom of God."

Then he got into the boat and his disciples followed him. There were also other boats with him. As they sailed, he fell asleep in the stern on a cushion.

Without warning a furious squall came down on the lake, so that the boat was being swamped, and they were in great danger. The disciples went and woke him, saying, "Lord. Save is! Don't you care if we drown?" He replied, "You of little faith, why are you so afraid?"

He got up, rebuked the wind and said to the waves, "Quiet! Be still!" Then the wind died down and it was completely calm.

He said to his disciples, "Why are you so afraid? Do you still have not faith?" They were terrified and in amazement they asked one another, "Who is this? He commands even the winds and the water, and they obey him!"[1]

(Mt. 8:28-34 / Mk. 5:1-20 / Lk. 8:26-39)

They went across the lake to the region of the [*Gadarenes*] Gerasenes when Jesus got out of the boat and stepped ashore, two demon-possessed men of the town coming from the tombs met him. They were so violent that no one could pass that way.

[*The following is the description of one of them by Mark and Luke:*]

For a long time this man[2] had not worn clothes or lived in a house, but had lived in the tombs. No one could bind him any more, not even with a chain. He had often be enchained hand and foot, but he tore the chains apart and broke the irons of his feet and had been driven by the demon into solitary places. No one was strong enough to subdue him. Night and day among the tombs and in the hills he would cry out and cut himself with stones.

When he saw Jesus from a distance, he ran and fell on his knees in front of him. Jesus had said to him, "Come out of this man, you evil spirit!" He cried out and fell at his feet, shouting at the top of his voice, "What do you want with me, Jesus, Son of the Most High God? Have you come here to torture us before the appointed time? Swear to God that you won't torture me!"

Jesus asked him, "What is your name?"

"My name is Legion," he replied, "for we are many." They begged him repeatedly not to order them to go into the Abyss and he begged Jesus again and again not to send them out of the area. Some distance from them a large herd of pigs was feeding on the nearby hillside. The demons begged Jesus, "If you drive us out, send us into the herd of pigs." He said to them, "Go!"

When the demons came out of the man, they went into the pigs, and the herd rushed down the steep bank into the lake and was drowned.

When those tending the pigs saw what had happened, they ran off and reported all this, including what had happened to the demon possessed men in the town and countryside and the people went out to see what had happened. When they came to Jesus, they saw the man who had been possessed by the legion of demons, sitting there, dressed and in his right mind; and they were afraid. Those who had seen it told the people what had happened to the demon-possessed man – and told about the pigs as well. Then all the people of the region of the Gerasenes began to plead with Jesus to leave their region because they were overcome with fear.

As Jesus was getting into the boat, the man who had been demon-possessed begged to go with him. Jesus did not let him, but said, "Go home to your family and tell them how much the Lord has done for you, and how he had had mercy on you." So the man went away and told all over the town and in the Decapolis how much Jesus had done for him. And all the people were amazed.

STUDY NOTES

1. Jesus calms the down the wind and the sea again for the second time in Chapter 16 Study Note No.: 4.

2. Mathew tells us that there were two men who were possessed. But Mark and Luke tell us about only one man. Therefore we understand that there were actually two devil possessed men who were both violent (Mt. 8:28), Luke and Mark give us detailed account of one of those men who probably was more violent than the other. For another example of such narration see Chapter 21 Study Note No.: 4.

XIII

POWERFUL MINISTRY OF JESUS CHRIST AND THE DOUBTS OF JOHN THE BAPTIST

(Mt. 9:1,18-26 / Mk. 5:21-43 / Lk. 8: 40-56)

When Jesus had again crossed over by boat and came to his own town on the other side of the lake, a crowd welcomed him, for they were all expecting him. A large crowd gathered around him while he was by the lake then a man named Jairus, a ruler of the synagogue came there, seen Jesus, he fell at his feet and pleaded earnestly with him, "My little daughter is dying. Please come and put your hands on her so that she will be healed and live." Jesus got up and went with him, and so did his disciples. A large crowd followed and pressed around him.

And a woman was there who had been subject to bleeding for twelve years. She had suffered a great deal under the care of many doctors and had spent all she had, yet instead of getting better she grew worse. When she heard about Jesus, she came up behind him in the crowd and touched the edge of his cloak, because she thought, "If I just touch his clothes, I will be healed." Immediately her bleeding stopped and she felt in her body that she was freed from her suffering.

At once Jesus realized that power had gone out from him. He turned around in the crowd and asked, "Who touched my clothes?" When they all denied it, Peter said, "Master, the people are crowding and pressing against you." But Jesus said, "Someone touched me; I know that power has gone, out from me."

But Jesus kept looking around to see who had done it. Then the woman, knowing what had happened to her, seeing that she could not go unnoticed, came trembling and fell at his feet. In the presence of all the people, she told why she had touched him and how she had been instantly healed. Then he said to her, "Take heart daughter, your faith has healed you. Go in peace and be freed from your suffering."

While Jesus was still speaking, some men came from the house of Jairus, the synagogue ruler. "Your daughter is dead," they said. "Why bother the teacher any more?"

Ignoring what they said, Jesus told the synagogue ruler, "Don't be afraid; just believe and she will be healed."

When he arrived at the house of Jairus, he did not let anyone go in with him except Peter, John and James, and the child's father and mother. Meanwhile, all the people were wailing and mourning for her. " Go away. Stop wailing," Jesus said. "She is not dead but asleep."

They laughed at him, knowing that she was dead. After he put them all out, he took the child's father and mother and the disciples who were with him and went in where the child was. He took her by the hand and said to her, "Talithakoum!" (which means, "Little girl, I say to you, get up!")Her spirit retuned at once. Immediately the girl stood up and walked around (she was twelve years old). At this they were completely astonished. But he gave strict orders not to let anyone know about this, and told them to give her something to eat. News of this spread through all that region.

(Mt. 9:27-35)

As Jesus went on from there, two blind men followed him, calling out, "Have mercy on us, Son of David!"

When he had gone indoors, the blind men came to him, and he asked them, "Do you believe that I am able to do this?"

"Yes, Lord," they replied.

Then he touched their eyes and said, "According to your faith will it be done to you"; and their sight was restored. Jesus warned them sternly, "See that no one knows about this." But they went out and spread the news about him all over that region.

While they [*the blind men*] were going out, a man who was demon-possessed and could not talk was brought to Jesus. And when the demon was driven out, the man who had been mute spoke. The crowd was amazed and said, "Nothing like this has ever been seen in Israel."

But the Pharisees said, "It is by the prince of demons that he drives out demons."[1]

Jesus went through all the towns and villages, teaching in their synagogues, preaching the good news of the kingdom and healing every disease and sickness.

(Mt. 11:2-19 / Lk. 7:18-35, 16:16)

John's disciples told him in prison about all these things. Calling two of them, he sent them to the Lord to ask, "Are you the one who was to come, or should we expect someone else?"

When the men came to Jesus, they said, "John the Baptist sent us to you to ask, 'Are you the one who was to come, or should we expect someone else?'"

At that very time Jesus cured many who had diseases, sicknesses and evil spirits, and gave sight to many who were blind. So he replied to the messengers, "Go back and report to John what you have seen and heard: The blind receive sight, the lame walk, those who have leprosy are cured, the deaf hear, the dead are raised, and the good news is preached to the poor. Blessed is the man who does not fall away on account of me."

After John's messengers left, Jesus began to speak to the crowd about John[2]: "What did you go out into the desert to see? A reed swayed by the wind? If not, what did you go out to see? A man dressed in fine clothes? No, those who wear expensive clothes and indulge in luxury are in palaces. But what did you go out to see? A prophet? Yes, I tell you, and more than a prophet. This is the one about whom it is written:

" 'I will send my messenger ahead of you,

who will prepare your way before you.'

"I tell you the truth, among those born of women there has not risen anyone greater than John the Baptist; yet the one who is least in the kingdom of God is greater than he.

"From the days of John the Baptist until now, the good news of kingdom of heaven is being preached and has been forcefully advancing, and everyone is forcing his way into it and forceful men lay hold of it. For all the Prophets and the Law prophesied until John. And if you are willing to accept it, he is the Elijah who was to come. He who has ears, let him hear."

(All the people, even the tax collectors, when they heard Jesus' words, acknowledged that God's way was right, because they had been baptized by John. But the Pharisees and experts in the law rejected God's purpose for themselves, because they had not been baptized by John.)

"To what, then, can I compare the people of this generation? What are they like? They are like children sitting in the marketplace and calling out to each other:

" 'We played the flute for you,

and you did not dance;

we sang a dirge,

and you did not cry.'

For John the Baptist came neither eating bread, nor drinking wine, and you say, 'He has a demon.' The Son of Man came eating and drinking, and you say, 'Here is a glutton and a drunkard, a friend of tax collectors and "sinners." But wisdom is proved right by all her children."

(Lk. 7:36-50)

Now one of the Pharisees invited Jesus to have dinner with him, so he went to the Pharisee's house and reclined at the table. When a woman who had lived a sinful life in that town learned that Jesus was eating at the Pharisee's house, she brought an alabaster jar of perfume, and as she stood behind him at his feet weeping, she began to wet his feet with her tears. Then she wiped them with her hair, kissed them and poured perfume on them[3].

When the Pharisee who had invited him saw this, he said to himself, "If this man were a prophet, he would know who is touching him and what kind of woman she is– that she is a sinner."

Jesus answered him, "Simon, I have something to tell you."

"Tell me, teacher," he said.

"Two men owed money to a certain moneylender. One owed him five hundred denarii, and the other fifty. Neither of them had the money to pay him back, so he canceled the debts of both. Now which of them will love him more?"

Simon replied, "I suppose the one who had the bigger debt canceled."

"You have judged correctly," Jesus said.

Then he turned toward the woman and said to Simon, "Do you see this woman? I came into your house. You did not give me any water for my feet, but she wet my feet with her tears and wiped them with her hair. You did not give me a kiss, but this woman, from the time I entered, has not stopped kissing my feet. You did not put oil on my head, but she has poured perfume on my feet. Therefore, I tell you, her many sins have been forgiven – for she loved much. But he who has been forgiven little loves little."

Then Jesus said to her, "Your sins are forgiven."

The other guests began to say among themselves, "Who is this who even forgives sins?"

Jesus said to the woman, "Your faith has saved you; go in peace."

STUDY NOTES

1. This is the second incidence of the Pharisees passing such a comment and this time Jesus does not respond to their comment. Chapter 10 Study Note No: 5.

2. This is the second time that Jesus gives testimony about John the Baptist
   First time Chapter 7 Study Note No: 3.
   Third time Chapter 18 Study Note No: 7.
   Fourth time Chapter 26 Study Note No: 3.

3. She is the first woman to pay her respects in this manner. The other woman is Mary as seen in Chapter 26 Study Note No: 2

XIV
THE MINISTERIAL JOURNEY CONTINUES VIA NAZARETH

(Mt. 13:53-58 / Mk. 6:1-6 / Lk. 4:16-30)

He went to Nazareth, where he had been brought up, accompanied by his disciples and on the Sabbath day he went into the synagogue, as was his custom. And he stood up to read. The scroll of the prophet Isaiah was handed to him. Unrolling it, he found the place where it is written:

"The Spirit of the Lord is on me,

because he has anointed me

to preach good news to the poor.

He has sent me to proclaim freedom for the

Prisoners

and recovery of sight for the blind,

to release the oppressed,

to proclaim the year of the Lord's favor."

Then he rolled up the scroll, gave it back to the attendant and sat down. The eyes of everyone in the synagogue were fastened on him, and he began by saying to them, "Today this scripture is fulfilled in your hearing."

All spoke well of him and were amazed at the gracious words that came from his lips. "Where did this man get all these things?" they asked. "What's this wisdom that has been given him, that he even does miracles! Where did this man get this wisdom and these miraculous powers? Isn't this the carpenter? Isn't this son of Joseph, the carpenter? Isn't his mother's name Mary, and aren't his brothers James, Joseph, Simon and Judas? Aren't all his sisters with us? And they took offense at him.

Jesus said to them, "Surely you will quote this proverb to me: 'Physician, heal yourself! Do here in your hometown, what we have heard that you did in Capernaum.'"

"I tell you the truth," Jesus said to them, "Only in his home town among his relatives and in his own house is a prophet without honor."

(Because of their lack of faith, he could not do any miracles there, except lay his hands on a few sick people and heal them.)

"I assure you," Jesus continued, "that there were many widows in Israel in Elijah's time, when the sky was shut for three and a half years and there was a severe famine throughout the land. Yet Elijah was not sent to any of them, but to a widow in Zarephath in the region of Sidom. And there were many in Israel with leprosy in the time of Elisha the prophet, yet not one of them was cleansed –only Naaman the Syrian."

All the people in the synagogue were furious when they heard this. They got up, drove him out of the town, and took him to the brow of the hill on which the town was built, in order to throw him down the cliff [1]. But he walked right through the crowd and went on his way. Jesus was amazed at their lack of faith, and he went around teaching from village to village.

(Lk. 8: 1-3)

After this, Jesus traveled about from one town and village to another, proclaiming the good news of the kingdom of God. The Twelve were with him, and also some women who had been cured of evil spirits and diseases: Mary (called Magdalene) from whom seven demons had come out; Joanna the wife of Cuza, the manager of Herod's household; Susanna; and many others. These women were helping to support them out of their own means.

STUDY NOTES

1. Second unsuccessful attempt to kill Jesus.
   First unsuccessful attempt Chapter 3 Study Note No: 2.
   Third unsuccessful attempt Chapter 19 Study Note No: 4.
   Fourth unsuccessful attempt Chapter 19 Study Note No: 8.

XV

THE HARVEST IS PLENTIFUL BUT THE WORKERS ARE FEW

(Mt. 9:36-11:1 / Mk. 6:7-13 / Lk. 9:1-6, 12:2-9, 11, 12, 49-53)

When he saw the crowds, he had compassion on them, because they were harassed and helpless, like sheep without a shepherd. Then he said to his disciples, "The harvest is plentiful but the workers are few. Ask the Lord of the harvest, therefore, to sent out workers into his harvest field."

He called his twelve disciples to him and gave them power and authority to drive out evil spirits and to heal every disease and sickness.

These are the names of the twelve apostles:[1]

1. First, **Simon** (who is called Peter) and

2. His brother **Andrew**;

3. **James** son of Zebedee, and

4. his brother **John**;

5. **Philip** and

6. **Bartholomew**;

7. **Thomas** and

8. **Matthew** the tax collector;

9. **James** son of Alphaeus, and

10. **Thaddaeus**;

11. **Simon** the Zealot and

12. **Judas Iscariot**, who betrayed him.

He sent them out to preach the kingdom of God and to heal the sick with the following instructions:[2] "Do not go among the Gentiles or enter any town of the Samaritans. Go rather to the lost sheep of Israel. As you go, preach this message: 'The kingdom of heaven is near.' Heal the sick, raise the dead, cleanse those who have leprosy, drive out demons. Freely you have received, freely give. Do not take along any gold or silver or copper in your belts; take not bag nor bread for the journey, or extra tunic, or sandals or a staff; for the worker is worth his keep.

"Take nothing for the journey except a staff and wear sandals. Whatever town or village you enter, search for some worthy person there and stay at his house until you leave. As you enter the home, give it your greeting. If the home is deserving, let your peace rest on it; if it is not, let your peace return to you. If anyone will not welcome you or listen to your words, shake the dust off your feet when you leave that home or town. I tell you the truth, it will be more bearable for Sodom and Gomorrah on the Day of Judgment than for that town. I am sending you out like sheep among wolves. Therefore be as shrewd as snakes and as innocent as doves.

"Be on your guard against men; they will hand you over to the local councils and flog you in their synagogues. On my account you will be brought before governors and kings as witnesses to them and to the Gentiles. When you are brought before synagogues rulers and authorities, do not worry about how you will defend yourselves or what you will say. At that time you will be given what to say, for it will not be you speaking, but the Spirit of your Father speaking through you.

"Brother will betray brother to death, and a father his child; children will rebel against their parents and have them put to death. All men will hate you because of me, but he who stands firm to the end will be saved. When you are persecuted in one place, flee to another. I tell you the truth, you will not finish going through the cities of Israel before the Son of Man comes.

"A student is not above his teacher, nor servant above his master. It is enough for the student to be like his teacher, and the servant like his master. If the head of the house has been called Beelzebub, how much more the members of his household!

"So do not be afraid of them. There is nothing concealed that will not be disclosed, or hidden that will not be made known. What I tell you in the dark, speak in the daylight; what is whispered in your ear, proclaim from the roofs. I tell you, my friends, do not be afraid of those who kill the body but cannot kill the soul. But I will show you whom you should fear: Be afraid of the One who can destroy both soul and body in hell. Yes, I tell you, fear him. Are not two sparrows sold for a penny? Yet not one of them will fall to the ground apart from the will of your Father. Not one of them is forgotten by God. And even the very hairs of your head are all numbered. So don't be afraid; you are worth more than many sparrows.

"Whoever acknowledges me before men, I will also acknowledge him before my Father in heaven. But whoever disowns me before men, I will disown him before my Father in heaven.

"I have come to bring fire on the earth, and how I wish it were already kindled! But I have baptism to undergo, and how distressed I am until it is completed!

"Do not suppose that I have come to bring peace to the earth. I did not come to bring peace, but a sword. From now on there will be five in one family divided against each other, three against two and two against three. For I have come to turn

" 'a man against his father,

a daughter against her mother,

a daughter-in-law against her mother-in-law –

a man's enemies will be the members of his

own household.'

"Anyone who loves his father or mother more than me is not worthy of me; anyone who loves his son or daughter more than me is not worthy of me; and anyone who does not take his cross and follow me is not worthy of me. Whoever finds his life will lose it, and whoever loses his life for my sake will find it.

"He who receives you receives me, and he who receives me receives the one who sent me. Anyone who receives a prophet because he is a prophet will receive a prophet's reward, and anyone who receives a righteous man because he is a righteous man will receive a righteous man's reward. And if anyone gives even a cup of cold water to one of these little ones because he is my disciple, I tell you the truth, he will certainly not lose his reward."

After Jesus had finished instructing his twelve disciples he sent them out two by two. He went on from there to teach and preach in the towns of Galilee.

So they set out and went from village to village, and preached that people should repent. They drove out many demons and anointed many sick people with oil and healed them.

STUDY NOTES

1. This is the list of apostles sent out for ministry. Chapter 9 Study Note No: 1.

2. When Jesus sent out disciples again for the second time later in His ministry, then too He gave them similar instructions. See Chapter 4 Study Note No: 2 .

XVI
THE EXECUTION OF JOHN THE BAPTIST

(Mt. 14:1-3 & 6-12 / Mk. 6:14-16 & 19-29 / Lk. 9:7-9)

[As Jesus ministry was progressing in Galilee the following happened to John the Baptist in Judea]

Herod had arrested John and bound him and put him in prison because of Herodias, his brother Philip's wife. Herodias nursed a grudge against John and wanted to kill him. But she was not able to, because Herod feared John and protected him, knowing him to be a righteous and holy man. When Herod heard John, he was greatly puzzled; yet he liked to listen to him.

Finally the opportune time came. On his birthday Herod gave a banquet for is high officials and military commanders and the leading men of Galilee. When the daughter of Herodias came in and danced, she pleased Herod and his dinner guests.

The king said to the girl, "Ask me for anything you want, and I'll give it to you." And he promised her with an oath, "Whatever you ask I will give you, up to half my kingdom."

She went out and said to her mother, "What shall I ask for?"

"The head of John the Baptist," she answered.

At once the girl hurried in to the king with the request: "I want you to give me right now the head of John the Baptist on a platter."

The king was greatly distressed, but because of his oaths and his dinner guests, he did not want to refuse her. So he immediately sent an executioner with orders to bring John's head. The man went, beheaded John in the prison, and brought back his head on a platter. He presented it to the girl, and she gave it to her mother. On hearing of this, John's disciples came and took his body and laid it in a tomb.

At that time [*When John the Baptist was thus killed,*] Herod the tetrarch heard[1] the reports about Jesus, for Jesus' name had become well known. He said to his attendants, "This is John the Baptist; he has risen from the dead! That is why miraculous powers are at work in him."

Herod the tetrarch was perplexed because some were saying that 'John had been raised from the dead' others that 'Elijah had appeared',

and still others that 'one of the prophets of long ago had come back to life'.

But when Herod heard this, he said, "John, the man I beheaded, has been raised from the dead! I beheaded John. Who, then, is this I hear such things about?" And he tried to see him.

(Mt. 14:12-21 / Mk. 6:30-44 / Lk. 9:10-17 / Jn. 6:1-15)

[*John's disciples buried his body,*] then they went and told Jesus. The apostles gathered around Jesus[2] and reported to him all they had done and taught. Then, because so many people were coming and going that they did not even have a chance to eat, he said to them, "Come with me by yourselves to a quiet place and get some rest."

He withdrew by boat privately then he took them with him and they withdrew by themselves in a boat and crossed to the far shore of the Sea of Galilee (that is, the Sea of Tiberias) to a solitary place in a town called Bethsaida.

And a great crowd of people followed him because they saw the miraculous signs he had performed on the sick. Many who saw them leaving recognized them and ran on foot from all the towns and got there ahead of them. When Jesus landed and saw a large crowd, he had compassion on them, because they were like sheep without a shepherd and he welcomed them. Then Jesus went upon a mountainside and sat down with his disciples. The Jewish Passover Feast was near[3]. He spoke to them about the kingdom of God and began teaching them many things. He healed those who needed healing.

Late in the day as evening approached the twelve came to him and said, "Send the crowd so they can go to the surrounding villages and countryside and find food and lodging, because we are in a remote place here and its already very late."

Jesus replied, "They do not need to go away. You give them something to eat."

When Jesus looked up and saw a great crowd coming toward him, he said to Philip, "Where shall we buy bread for these people to eat?" He asked this only to test him, for he already had in mind what he was going to do.

Philip answered him, "Eight months' wages would not buy enough bread for each one to have a bite! Are we to go and spend that much on bread and give it to them to eat?"

"How many loaves do you have?" he asked. "Go and see."

Another of his disciples, Andrew, Simon Peter's brother, spoke up, "Here is a boy with five small barley loaves and two small fish, but how far will they go among so many?" "Bring them here to me." he said. Then Jesus directed them to have all the people sit down in groups of fifty each on the green grass. There was plenty of grass in that place and they sat down in groups of hundreds and fifties.

Taking the five loaves and the two fish and looking up to heaven, he gave thanks and broke them. Then he gave them to the disciples to set before the people and the disciples gave them to the people. He also divided the two fish among them all.

When they had all had enough to eat, he said to his disciples, "Gather the pieces that are left over. Let nothing be waste." So they gathered them and filled twelve baskets with the pieces of the five barley loaves left over by those who had eaten. The number of those who ate was about five thousand men, besides women and children.

After the people saw the miraculous sign that Jesus did, they began to say, "Surely this is the Prophet who is to come into the world." Jesus, knowing that they intended to come and make him king by force, withdrew again to a mountain by himself.

(Mt. 14:22-34 / Mk. 6:45-53 / Jn. 6:16-21)

When evening came, Jesus made the disciples get into the boat and go on ahead of him to Bethsaida on the other side, while he dismissed the crowd. His disciples went down to the lake, where they got into a boat and set off across the lake for Capernaum. By now it was dark. After he had dismissed them, he went up on a mountainside by himself to pray. When evening came, he was there alone, but the boat was already a considerable distance from land, buffeted by the waves because the wind was against it. A strong wind was blowing and the waters grew rough. He saw the disciples straining at the oars, because the wind was against them. When they had rowed three or three and a half miles, about the fourth watch of the night they saw Jesus approaching the boat, walking on the water. He was about to pass by them.

When the disciples saw him walking on the lake, they were terrified. "It's a ghost," they said, and cried out in fear.

But Jesus immediately said to them: "Take courage! It is I. don't be afraid." Then they were willing to take him into the boat

."Lord, if it's you," Peter replied, "tell me to come to you on the water."

"Come," he said.

Then Peter got down out of the boat, walked on the water and came toward Jesus. But when he saw the wind, he was afraid and, beginning to sink, cried out, "Lord, save me!"

Immediately Jesus reached out his hand and caught him. "You of little faith," he said, "why did you doubt?"

And when they climbed into the boat, the wind died down[4]. Then those who were in the boat worshiped him, saying, "Truly you are the Son of God." For they had not understood about the loaves; their hearts were hardened. When they had crossed over, they landed at Gennesaret and anchored there.

(Mt. 14:35,36 / Mk. 6:54-56)

As soon as they got out of the boat, the men of that place recognized Jesus, they sent word to all the surround country. They ran throughout the whole region and carried the sick on mats to wherever they heard he was. People brought all their sick to him. And wherever he went – into villages, towns or countryside – they place the sick in the marketplaces. They begged him to let them touch even the edge of his cloak, and all who touched him were healed.

(Jn. 6: 22-71)

The next day the crowd that had stayed on the opposite shore of the lake realized that only one boat had been there, and that Jesus had not entered it with his disciples, but that they had gone away alone. Then some boats from Tiberias landed near the place where the people had eaten the bread after the Lord had given thanks. Once the crowd realized that neither Jesus nor his disciples were there, they got into the boats and went to Capernaum in search of Jesus.

When they found him on the other side of the lake, they asked him, "Rabbi, when did you get here?"

Jesus answered, "I tell you the truth, you are looking for me, not because you saw miraculous signs but because you ate the loaves and had your fill. Do not work for food that spoils, but for food that endures to eternal life, which the Son of Man will give you. On him God the Father has placed his seal of approval."

Then they asked him, "What must we do to do the works God requires?"

Jesus answered, "The work of God is this: to believe in the one he has sent."

So they asked him, "What miraculous sign then will you give that we may see it and believe you? What will you do? Our forefathers ate the manna in the desert; as it is written: 'He gave them bread from heaven to eat.'"

Jesus said to them, "I tell you truth, it is not Moses who has given you the bread from heaven, but it is my Father who gives you the true bread from heaven. For the bread of God is he who comes down from heaven and gives life to the world."

"Sir," they said, "from now on give us this bread."

Then Jesus declared, "I am the bread of life. He who comes to me will never go hungry, and he who believes in me will never be thirsty. But as I told you, you have seen me and still you do not believe. All that the Father gives me will come to me, and whoever comes to me I will never drive away. For I have come down from heaven not to do my will but to do the will of him who sent me. And this is the will of him who sent me, which I shall lose none of all that he has given me, but raise them up at the last day. For my Father's will is that everyone who looks to the Son and believes in him shall have eternal life, and I will raise him up at the last day."

At this the Jews began to grumble about him because he said, "I am the bread that came down from heaven." They said, "Is this not Jesus, the son of Joseph, whose father and mother we know? How can he now say, 'I came down from heaven'?"

"Stop grumbling among yourselves," Jesus answered. "No one can come to me unless the Father who sent me draws him, and I will raise him up at the last day. It is written in the Prophets: 'They will all be taught by God.' Everyone who listens to the Father and learns from him comes to me. No one has seen the Father except the one who is from God; only he has seen the Father. I tell you the truth, he who believes has everlasting life. I am the bread of life. Your forefathers ate the manna in the desert, yet they died. But here is the bread that comes down from heaven, which a man may eat and not die. I am the living bread that came down from heaven. If anyone eats of this bread, he will live forever. This bread is my flesh, which I will give for the life of the world."

Then the Jews began to argue sharply among themselves, "How can this man give us his flesh to eat?"

Jesus said to them, "I tell you the truth, unless you eat the flesh of the Son of Man and drink his blood, you have no life in you. Whoever eats my flesh and drinks my blood has eternal life, and I will raise him up at the last day. For my flesh is real food and my blood is real drink. Whoever eats my flesh and drinks my blood remains in me, and I in him. Just as the living Father sent me and I live because of the Father, so the one who feeds on me will live because of me. This is the bread that came down from heaven. Your forefathers ate manna and died, but he who feeds on this bread will live forever." He said this while teaching in the synagogue in Capernaum.

On hearing it, many of his disciples said, "This is a hard teaching. Who can accept it?"

Aware that his disciples were grumbling about this, Jesus said to them, "Does this offend you? What if you see the Son of Man ascend to where he was before! The Spirit gives life; the flesh counts for nothing. The words I have spoken to you are spirit and they are life. Yet there are some of you who do not believe." For Jesus had known from the beginning which of them did not believe and who would betray him. He went on to say, "This is why I told you that no one can come to me unless the Father has enabled him."

From this time many of his disciples turned back and no longer followed him.[*These were the very same people who wanted to make him king!*]

"You do not want to leave too, do you?" Jesus asked the Twelve.

Simon Peter answered him, "Lord, to whom shall we go? You have the words of eternal life. We believe and know that you are the Holy One of God."[5]

Then Jesus replied, "Have I not chosen you, the Twelve? Yet one of you is a devil" (He meant Judas, the Son of Simon Iscariot, who though one of the Twelve, was later to betray him).

STUDY NOTES

1. Herod who had murdered John the Baptist hears the reports about Jesus. This could be a result of the wider ministerial campaign that Jesus conducted by sending out His twelve disciples two by two. So by now, news about Jesus was being discussed by the governor of the land!
2. The following is the sequence in which the events took place:
    a) Jesus sends out his twelve disciples two by two for ministry.
    b) Herod executes John the Baptist.
    c) Herod learns about Jesus' ministry.
    d) John's disciples inform Jesus of John's death.
    e) The twelve apostles return back to Jesus after their ministry.
3. This is the third Passover feast during Jesus' ministry.
    First Passover Chapter 5 Study Note No: 1
    Second Passover Chapter 8 Study Note No: 1
    Fourth Passover Chapter 22 Study Note No: 2
    Jesus is entering His last year of ministry. He is crucified in the next Passover feast.
4. This is second incidence of the wind being calmed by Jesus.
    See Chapter 12 Study Note No: 1
5. This is the first time Peter proclaims Jesus to be the 'Christ'. See Chapter 17 Study Note No: 5

THE FINAL YEAR OF CHRIST'S MINISTRY

XVII

THE FIRST PART OF THE FINAL YEAR

[(Jn. 6: 4)

The Jewish Passover Feast was near.[1]

(Jn. 7: 1)

After this, Jesus went around in Galilee, purposely staying away from Judea because the Jews there were waiting to take his life. In Galilee...]

(Mt. 15:1-20 / Mk. 7:1-23)

The Pharisees and some of the teachers of the law who had come from Jerusalem[2] gathered around Jesus[3] and saw some of his disciples eating food with hands that were "unclean," that is, unwashed. (The Pharisees and all the Jews do not eat unless they give their hands a ceremonial washing, holding to the tradition of the elders. When they come from the market place they do not eat unless they wash. And they observe many other traditions, such as the washing of cups, pitches and kettles.)

So the Pharisees and teachers of the law asked Jesus, "Why don't your disciples live according to the tradition of the elders instead of eating their food with 'unclean' hand?"

Jesus replied, "And why do you break the command of God for the sake of your tradition? For God said, 'Honor your father and mother' and 'Anyone who curses his father or mother must be put to death.' But you say that if a man says to his father or mother, 'Whatever help you might otherwise have received from me is Corban' (that is, a gift devoted to God), then you no longer let him do anything for his father or mother. Thus you nullify the word of God by your tradition that you have handed down. And you do many things like that. You hypocrites! Isaiah was right when he prophesied about you hypocrites as it is written:

" 'These people honor me with their lips,
but their hearts are far from me.
They worship me in vain;
their teachings are but rules taught by
men.'

"You have let go of the commands of God and are holding on to the traditions of men.

Again Jesus called the crowd to him and said, "Listen to me, everyone, and understand this. Nothing outside a man can make him 'unclean' by going into him. Rather, it is what comes out of a man that makes him 'unclean'. If any one has ears to hear, let him hear."

Then the disciples came to him and asked, "Do you know that the Pharisees were offended when they heard this?"

He replied, "Every plant that my heavenly Father has not planted will be pulled up by the roots. Leave them; they are blind guides. If a blind man leads a blind man, both will fall into a pit."

After he had left the crowd and entered the house, Peter said, "Explain the parable to us."

"Are you so dull?" Jesus asked them. "Don't you see that nothing that enters a man from the outside can make him 'unclean'? For it doesn't go into his heart but into his stomach, and then out of his body." (In saying this, Jesus declared all foods "clean.")

But the things that come out of the mouth come from the heart, and these make a man 'unclean.' For out of the heart come evil thoughts, murder, adultery, sexual immorality, theft, false testimony, greed, malice, deceit, lewdness, envy, slander, arrogance and folly. All these evils come from inside and make a man 'unclean', but eating with unwashed hands does not make him 'unclean'."

(Mt. 15:21-28 / Mk. 7:24-30)

Leaving that place, Jesus withdrew to the region of Tyre and Sidon. A Canaanite woman from that vicinity, whose little daughter was possessed by an evil spirit heard about him, came to him, crying out, "Lord, Son of David, have mercy on me! My daughter is suffering terrible from demon-possession."

Jesus did not answer a word. So his disciples came to him and urged him, "Send her away, for she keeps crying out after us."

He answered, "I was sent only to the lost sheep of Israel."

He entered a house and did not want anyone to know it; yet he could not keep his presence secret. The woman came and fell at his feet and knelt before him, "Lord, help me!" she said. The woman was a Greek, born in Syrian Phoenicia.

"First let the children eat all they want," he told her, "for it is not right to take the children's bread and toss it to their dogs."

"Yes, Lord," she replied, "but even the dogs under the table eat the children's crumbs."

Then Jesus answered, "Woman, you have great faith! For such a reply, you may go; the demon has left your daughter." And her daughter was healed from that very hour.

She went home and found her child lying on the bed, and the demon gone.

(Mk. 7: 31-37)

Then Jesus left the vicinity of Tyre and went through Sidon, down to the Sea of Galilee and into the region of the Decapolis. There some people brought to him a man who was deaf and could hardly talk, and they begged him to place his hand on the man.

After he took him aside, away from the crowd, Jesus put his fingers into the man's ears. The he spit and touched the man's tongue. He looked up to heaven and with a deep sigh said to him, "Ephphatha!" (Which means, "Be opened!"). At this, the man's ears were opened, his tongue was loosened and he began to speak plainly.

Jesus commanded them not to tell anyone. But the more he did so, the more they kept talking about it. People were overwhelmed with amazement. "He has done everything well," they said. "He even makes the deaf hear and the mute speak."

(Mt. 15:29-38 / Mk. 8:1-9)

Jesus left there and went along the Sea of Galilee. Then he went up on a mountainside and sat down. Great crowds came to him, bringing the lame, the blind, the crippled, the mute and many others, and laid them at his feet; and he healed them. Then people were amazed when they saw the mute speaking, the crippled made well, the lame walking and the blind seeing. And they praised the God of Israel.

During those days another large crowd gathered. Since they had nothing to eat, Jesus called his disciples to him and said, "I have compassion for these people; they have already been with me three days and have nothing to eat. I do not want to send them away hungry. If I send them home hungry, they will collapse on the way, because some of them have come a long distance."

His disciples answered, "Where could we get enough bread in this remote place to feed such a crowd?"

"How many loaves do you have?" Jesus asked.

" Seven," they replied, "and a few small fish."

He told the crowd to sit down on the ground. Then he took the seven loaves and the fish, and when he had given thanks, he broke them and gave them to the disciples to set before the people, and they did so. They all ate and were satisfied. Afterward the disciples picked up seven basketfuls of broken pieces that were left over. The number of those who ate was four thousand, besides women and children.

(Mt. 15:39-16:4 / Mk. 8:10-13 / Lk. 12:54-56)

After Jesus had sent the crowd away, he got into the boat with his disciples and went to the vicinity of Magadan [*Dalmanutha*]. The Pharisees came and began to question Jesus. To test him, they asked him for sign from heaven[4] He sighed deeply and said, "Why does this generation ask for a miraculous sign? When evening comes, you say, 'It will be fair weather, for the sky is red,' and in the morning, 'Today it will be stormy, for the sky is red and overcast.' You know how to interpret the appearance of the sky, but you cannot interpret the signs of the times. A wicked and adulterous generation looks for a miraculous sign, but none will be given it except the sign of Jonah." Then he left them, got back into the boat and crossed to the other side.

(Mt. 16:5-12 / Mk. 8:14-21 / Lk. 12:1)

When they went across the lake, the disciples forgot to take bread, except for one loaf they had with them in the boat.

Meanwhile, when a crowd a many thousands had gathered, so that they were trampling on one another, Jesus began to speak first to his disciples, saying: "Be on your guard against the yeast of the Pharisees and Sadducees, that of the Herod which is hypocrisy.

They discussed this among themselves and said, "It is because we didn't bring any bread."

Aware of their discussion, Jesus asked, "You of little faith, why are you talking among yourselves about having no bread? Do you still not understand? Are your hearts hardened? Do you have eyes but fail to see, and ears but fail to hear? And don't you remember? When I broke the five loaves for the five thousand, how many basketfuls of pieces did you pick up?"

"Twelve," they replied.

"And when I broke the seven loaves for the four thousand, how many basketfuls of pieces did you pick up?"

They answered, "Seven."

He said to them, "How is it you don't understand that I was not talking to you about bread, but against the teachings of the Pharisees and Sadducees."

Then they understood that he was not telling them to guard against the yeast used in bread, but against the teaching of the Pharisees and Sadducees.

(Mk. 8: 22-26)

They came to Bethsaida, and some people brought a blind man and begged Jesus to touch him. He took the blind man by the hand and led him outside the village. When he had spit on the man's eyes and put his hands on him, Jesus asked, "Do you see anything?"

He looked up and said, "I see people; they look like trees walking around."

Once more Jesus put his hands on the man's eyes. Then his eyes were opened, his sight was restored, and he saw everything clearly. Jesus sent him home, saying, "Don't go and tell any one in the village."

(Mt. 16:13-28 / Mk. 8:27-9:1 / Lk. 9:18-27)

Jesus and his disciples went on to the villages around Caesarea Philippi. On the way when Jesus was praying in private and his disciples were with him, he asked them, "Who do people say the Son of Man is?"

They replied, "Some say John the Baptist; others say Elijah; and still others, Jeremiah one of the prophets of long ago has come back to life."

"But what about you?" he asked, "Who do you say I am?" Simon Peter answered, "You are the Christ, the Son of the living God."[5]

Jesus replied, "Blessed are you, Simon son of Jonah, for this was not revealed to you by man, but by my Father in heaven. And I tell you that you are Peter, and on this rock I will build my church, and the gates of Hades will not overcome it. I will give you the keys of the kingdom of heaven; whatever you bind on earth will be bound in heaven, and whatever you loose on earth will loosed in heaven." Then he warned his disciples not to tell anyone that he was the Christ.

[6]From that time on Jesus began to explain to his disciples that he must go to Jerusalem and suffer many things and be rejected by the elders, chief priests and teachers of the law, and that he must be killed and on the third day be raised to life. He spoke plainly about this.

Peter took him aside and began to rebuke him. "Never, Lord!" he said. "This shall never happen to you...!"[7] But when Jesus turned and looked at his disciples, he rebuked Peter. "Get behind me, Satan! You are a stumbling block to me; you do not have in mind the things of God, but the things of men."

Then he called the crowd to him along with his disciples and said, "If anyone would come after me, he must deny himself and take up his cross daily and follow me. For whoever wants to save his life will lose it, but whoever loses his life for me and for the gospel will save it. What good will it be for a man if he gains the whole world, yet forfeits his soul?

"If anyone is ashamed of me and my words in this adulterous and sinful generation, the Son of Man will be ashamed of him when he comes in his glory and in the glory of the Father and of the holy angels and then he will reward each person according to what he has done. I tell you the truth, some who are standing here will not taste death before they see the Son of Man coming in his kingdom."

STUDY NOTES

1. There are no details of what happened during Jesus' visit to Jerusalem for the third Passover feast (Mar/Apr). But from (Jn. 7: 2) onwards John gives an account of Jesus' visit to Jerusalem for the Feast of Tabernacles (Sep/Oct)- six months later. From Jn. 7:1 we know that Jesus was purposely staying away from Judea because the Jews there were waiting to take His life. Therefore we conclude that His last visit to Jerusalem for the Passover feast was not a pleasant one. The following portion gives an account of what had happened in Galilee, during those six months i.e., after His

return from the Passover feast (Mar/Apr) and before the departure for the feast of Tabernacles (Sep/Oct).

2. The very same group of people who wanted to get Him killed is dinning with Him here!

3. This is the third and final time that such meeting taking place between Jesus and the leaders from Jerusalem. The others are as follows:
I. Chapter 6 Study note No: 1
II. Chapter 10 Study note No: 4

4. This is the second time such a sign is being sought. Chapter 10 Study note No:6. Jesus gives the appearance of the sky for those who sought a sign from heaven! It is to be noted that after talking about its interpretation, Jesus gives them the same sign He had given earlier – this time without much explanation.

5. This is the second time Peter calls Jesus as 'Christ'. Chapter 16 Study note No: 5.

6. Only from this point of His ministry, Jesus begins to talk about His death and resurrection.

7. The disciples who had fancied Jesus to be the one who is to deliver them politically are aghast at the prospect of Him getting killed by the Jews. Peter's reaction is an expression of this anguish.

XVIII
THE TRANSFIGURATION

(Mt. 17:1-21 / Mk. 9:2-29 / Lk. 9:28-45)

About six days[1] [*eight days*] after Jesus said this, he took Peter, James and John the brother of James with him and went up onto a high mountain to pray by themselves. As he was praying, he transfigured before them. The appearance of his face changed. His face shone like the sun and his clothes became dazzling white as white as the light bright as a flash of lightning. Whiter than anyone in the world could bleach them. Two men, Moses and Elijah, appeared in glorious splendor, talking with Jesus. They spoke about his departure, which he was about to bring to fulfillment at Jerusalem. Peter and his companions were very sleepy, but when they became fully awake, they saw his glory and the two men standing with him. As the men were leaving Jesus, Peter said to him, "Master, it is good for us to be here. If you wish, let us put up three shelters –one for you, one of Moses and one for Elijah." (He did not know what he was saying, they were so frightened.)

While he was still speaking, a bright cloud appeared and enveloped them, and they were afraid as they entered the cloud. A voice came from the cloud[2], saying, "This is my Son, whom I Love and whom I have chosen; listen to him." When the disciples heard this, they fell facedown to the ground, terrified. But Jesus came and touched them. "Get up," he said. "Don't be afraid." When they looked up, they saw no one except Jesus.[3]

The next day,[4] as they were coming down the mountain, Jesus gave them orders not to tell anyone what they had seen until the Son of Man had risen from the dead.[5] They kept the matter to themselves, discussing what "rising from the dead" meant.

And they asked him, "Why do the teachers of the law say that Elijah must come first?"

Jesus replied, "To be sure, Elijah does come first, and restores all things. Why then is it written that the Son of Man must suffer much and be rejected? But I tell you, Elijah has already come, and they did not recognize him. They have done to him everything they wished, just as it is written about him. In the same way the Son of Man is going to suffer at their hands."[6] Then the disciples understood that he was talking to them about John the Baptist[7].

When they came to the other disciples, they saw a large crowd around them and the teachers of the law arguing with them. As soon as all the people saw Jesus, they were overwhelmed with wonder and ran to greet him.

"What are you arguing with them about?" he asked.

A man in the crowd approached him and knelt before him and called out, "Teacher, I beg you to look at my son, for he is my only child. A spirit that has robbed him of speech seizes him and he suddenly screams. Whenever it seizes him, it throws him to the ground. He foams at the mouth gnashes his teeth and becomes rigid. It scarcely ever leaves him and is destroying him. I begged your disciples to drive it out, but they could not."

"O unbelieving and perverse generation," Jesus replied, "how long shall I stay with you? How long shall put up with you? Bring the boy to me."

So they brought him. When the spirit saw Jesus, it immediately threw the boy into a convulsion. He fell to the ground and rolled around, foaming at the mouth.

Jesus asked the boy's father, "How long has he been like this?"

"From childhood," he answered. "It is often thrown him into fire or water to kill him. But if you can do anything take pity on us and help us."

" 'If you can'?" said Jesus. "Everything is possible for him who believes."

Immediately the boy's father exclaimed, "I do believe, help me overcome my unbelief!"

When Jesus saw that a crowd was running to the scene, he rebuked the evil spirit. "You deaf and mute spirit," he said, "I command you, come out of him and never enter him again."

The spirit shrieked, convulsed him violently and came out. The boy looked so much like a corpse that many said, "He's dead." But Jesus took him by the hand and lifted him to his feet, and he stood up. Jesus gave him back to his father.

And they were all amazed at the greatness of God. While everyone was marveling at all that Jesus did, he said to his disciples, "Listen carefully to what I am about to tell you: The Son of Man is going to be betrayed into the hands of men."[8] But they did not understand what this meant[9].It was hidden from them, so that they did not grasp it, and they were afraid to ask him about it.

After Jesus had gone indoors, his disciples asked him privately, "Why couldn't we drive it out?"

He replied, "Because you have so little faith. I tell you the truth, if you have faith as small as a mustard seed, you can say to this mountain, 'Move from here to there' and it will move. Nothing will be impossible for you. This kind does not go out except by prayer and fasting."

(Mt. 17:22-27 / Mk. 9:30-32)

They left that place and passed through Galilee. Jesus did not want anyone to know where they were, because when they came together in Galilee, he taught his disciples and said to them, "The Son of Man is going to be betrayed into the hands of men. They will kill him, and after three days he will rise." But they did not understand what he meant and were afraid to ask him about it.[10]

After Jesus and his disciples arrived in Capernaum, the collectors of the two-drachma tax came to Peter and asked, "Doesn't your teacher pay the temple tax?"

"Yes, he does," he replied.

When Peter came into the house, Jesus was the first to speak. "What do you think, Simon?" he asked. "From whom do the kings of the earth collect duty and taxes –from their own sons or from others?"

"From others," Peter answered.

"Then he sons are exempt," Jesus said to him. "But so that we may not offend them, go to the lake and throw out your line. Take the first fish you catch; open its mouth and you will find a four-drachma coin. Take it and give it to them for my tax and yours."

(Mt. 18:1-35 / Mk. 9:33-50 / Lk. 9:46-50, 17:1-10)

At that time the disciples came to Jesus and asked, "Who is the greatest in the kingdom of heaven?"

He asked them, "What were you arguing about on the road?" But they kept quite because on the way they had argued about who was the greatest.

Sitting down, Jesus called the Twelve and said, "If anyone wants to be first, he must be the very last, and the servant of all."

He took a little child and had him stand among them. Taking him in his arms, he said to them.

And he said: "I tell you the truth, unless you change and become like little children, you will never enter the kingdom of heaven. Therefore, whoever humbles himself like this child is the greatest in the kingdom of heaven.

"Whoever welcomes one of these little children in my name welcomes me; and whoever welcomes me does not welcome me but the one who sent me."

"Teacher," said John, "we saw a man driving out demons in your name and we told him to stop, because he was not one of us."

"Do not stop him," Jesus said. "No one who does a miracle in my name can in the next moment say anything bad about me, for whoever is not against us is for us. I tell you the truth, anyone who gives you a cup of water in my name because you belong to Christ will certainly not lose his reward.

"And if anyone causes one of these little ones who believe in me to sin, it would be better for him to be drowned in the depths of the sea with a large millstone tied around his neck.

"Woe to the world because of the things that cause people to sin! Such things must come, but woe to the man through whom they come!

"If your hand causes you to sin, cut it off and throw it away. It is better for you to enter life maimed than with two hands to go into hell, where the fire never goes out. Where their worm does not die and the fire is not quenched and if your foot causes you to sin, cut it off and throw it away. It is better for you to enter life crippled than to have two feet and be thrown into hell Where their worm does not die and the fire is not quenched. And if your eye causes you to sin, pluck it out and throw it away. It is better for you to enter the kingdom of God with one eye than to have two eyes and be thrown into hell, where

" 'their worm does not die,

and the fire is not quenched.'

"See that you do not look down on one of these little ones. For I tell you that their angels in heaven always see the face of my Father in heaven. The Son of Man come to save what was lost.

"What do you think? If a man owns a hundred sheep,[11] and one of them wanders away, will he not leave the ninety-nine on the hills and go to look for the one that wandered off? And if he finds it, I tell you the truth, he is happier about that one sheep than about the ninety-nine that did not wander off. In the same way your Father in heaven is not willing that any of these little ones should be lost.

"So watch yourselves. If your brother sins against you, go and show him his fault, just between the two of you. If he listens to you, you have won your brother over. But if he will not listen, take one or two others along, so that 'every matter may be established by the testimony of two or three witnesses.' If he refuses to listen to them, tell it to the church; and if he refuses to listen even to the church, treat him as you would a pagan or a tax collector.

"I tell you the truth, whatever you bind on earth will be bound in heaven, and whatever you loose on earth will be loosed in heaven.

"Again, I tell you that if two of you on earth agree about anything you ask for, it will be done for you by my Father in heaven. For where two or three come together in my name, there am I with them."

Then Peter came to Jesus and asked, "Lord, how many times shall I forgive my brother when he sins against me? Up to seven times?"

Jesus answered, "I tell you, not seven times, but seventy times seven.

"Therefore, the kingdom of heaven is like a king who wanted to settle accounts with his servants. As he began the settlement, a man who owed him ten thousand talents was brought to him. Since he was not able to pay, the master ordered that he and his wife and his children and all that he had be sold to repay the debt.

"The servant fell on his knees before him. 'Be patient with me,' he begged, 'and I will pay back everything.' The servant's master took pity on him, canceled the debt and let him go.

"But when that servant went out, he found one of his fellow servants who owed him a hundred denarii. He grabbed him and began to choke him. 'Pay back what you owe me!' he demanded.

"His fellow servant fell to his knees and begged him, 'Be patient with me, and I will pay you back.'

"But he refused. Instead, he went off and had the man thrown into prison until he could pay the debt. When the other servants saw what had happened, they were greatly distressed and went and told their master everything that had happened.

"Then the master called the servant in. 'You wicked servant,' he said, 'I canceled all that debt of yours because you begged me to. Shouldn't you have had mercy on your fellow servant just as I had on you?' In anger his master turned him over to the jailers to be tortured, until he should pay back all the owed.

"This is how my heavenly Father will treat each of you unless you forgive your brother from your heart. Everyone will be salted with fire.

"Salt is good, but if it loses its saltiness, how can you make it salty again?[12] Have salt in yourselves, and beat peace with each other."

The apostles said to the Lord, "Increase our faith!"

He replied, "If you have faith as small as a mustard seed, you can say to this mulberry tree, 'Be uprooted and planted in the sea,' and it will obey you.

"Suppose one of you had a servant plowing or looking after the sheep, would he say to the servant when he comes in from the field, 'Come along now and sit down to eat'? Would he not rather say, 'Prepare my supper, get yourself ready and wait on me while I eat and drink; after that you may eat and drink'? Would he thank the servant because he did what he was told to do? So you also, when you have done everything you were told to do, should say, 'We are unworthy servants; we have only done our duty.'

STUDY NOTES

1. Though Matthew and Mark tell us that it was six days later, Luke puts it as eight days. Both of these could be right at the same time i.e., if the days of the previous incident and the next incident are taken into account, then the number of days become 'eight' at the same time, it is 'six days' if only the intermittent days are taken into account.

2. This is the second time in the life of Christ there is a voice from heaven.

First time Chapter 4 Study note No: 3

Third Time Chapter 27 Study note No: 9

3. It is important to note that John was an eyewitness to this incident. It is ironic that John is the only gospel writer who does not mention this at all!

Other similar cases where John is silent about are:

Chapter 21 Study note No: 2

Chapter 25 Study note No: 4

4. This incident of transfiguration must have happened in the night. The

following points endorse this view:

a) It is usual for Jesus to pray alone in the night.

b) We are told that the disciples were very sleepy and His clothes became dazzling white

5. For the second time Jesus talks about His resurrection.

6. For the third time Jesus is talking about His suffering and death.

7. This is the third time Jesus is referring to John the Baptist. The other places where He mentions of John are:

Chapter 7 Study note No: 3

Chapter 13 Study note No: 2

Chapter 26 Study note No: 3

8. This is the fourth time Jesus is talking about His death.

9. For the second time in succession the disciples neither understood nor get a clarification of what Jesus had said.

10. This passage is mentioning about the incident told earlier in Study Note No: 8

11. Jesus is using this parable for the second time in His ministry. See Chapter 7 Study note No: 5

12. Jesus uses the parable of salt-saltiness for the third time. Other places are:

Chapter 4 Study note No: 4

Chapter 9 Study note No: 3

XIX

THE FEAST OF TABERNACLES
IN JERUSALEM

(Jn. 7:1-11:54)

After this, Jesus went around in Galilee, purposely staying away from Judea because the Jews there were waiting to take his life.[1]

But when the Jewish Feast of Tabernacles was near, Jesus' brothers said to him, "You ought to leave here and go to Judea, so that your disciples may see the miracles you do. No one who wants to become a public figure acts in secret. Since you are doing these things, show yourself to the world." For even his own brothers did not believe in him.

Therefore Jesus told them, "The right time for me has not yet come; for you any time is right. The world cannot hate you, but it hates me because I testify that what it does is evil. You go to the Feast. I am not yet going up to this Feast, because for me the right time has not yet come." Having said this, he stayed in Galilee.

However, after his brothers had left for the Feast, he went also, not publicly, but in secret. Now at the Feast the Jews were watching for him and asking, "Where is that man?"

Among the crowds there was widespread whispering about him. Some said, "He is a good man."

Others replied, "No, he deceives the people." But no one would say anything publicly about him for fear of the Jews.

Not until halfway through the Feast did Jesus go up to the temple courts and begin to teach. The Jews were amazed and asked, "How did this man get such learning without having studied?"

Jesus answered, "My teaching is not my own. It comes from him who sent me. If anyone chooses to do God's will, he will find out whether my teaching comes from God or whether I speak on my own. He who speaks on his own does so to gain honor for himself, but he who works for the honor of the one who sent him is a man of truth; there is nothing false about him. Has not Moses given you the law? Yet not one of you keeps the law. Why are you trying to kill me?"

"You are demon-possessed," the crowd answered. "Who is trying to kill you?"

Jesus said to them, "I did one miracle, and you are all astonished. Yet, because Moses gave you circumcision (though actually it did not come from Moses, but from the patriarchs), you circumcise a child on the Sabbath. Now if a child can be circumcised on the Sabbath so that the law of Moses may not be broken, why are you angry with me for healing the whole man on the Sabbath? Stop judging by mere appearances, and make a right judgment."

At that point some of the people of Jerusalem began to ask, "Isn't this the man they are trying to kill?[2] Here he is, speaking publicly, and they are not saying a word to him. Have the authorities really concluded that he is the Christ? But we know where this man is from; when the Christ comes, no one will know where he is from."

Then Jesus, still teaching in the temple courts, cried out, "Yes, you know me, and you know where I am from. I am not here on my own, but he who sent me is true. You do not know him, but I know him because I am from him and he sent me."

At this they tried to seize him,[3] but no one laid a hand on him, because his time had not yet come.

[*The following is the description of the attempt*]

Still, many in the crowd put their faith in him. They said, "When the Christ comes, will he do more miraculous signs than this man?"

The Pharisees heard the crowd whispering such things about him. Then the chief priests and the Pharisees sent temple guards to arrest him.

Jesus said, "I am with you for only a short time, and then I go to the one who sent me. You will look for me, but you will not find me; and where I am, you cannot come."

The Jews said to one another, "Where does this man intend to go that we cannot find him? Will he go where our people live scattered among the Greeks, and teach the Greeks? What did he mean when he said, 'You will look for me, but you will not find me,' and 'where I am, you cannot come'?"

On the last and greatest day of the Feast, Jesus stood and said in loud voice, "If anyone is thirsty, let him come to me and drink. Whoever believes in me, as the Scripture has said, streams of living water will flow from within him." By this he meant the Spirit, whom those who believed in him were later to receive. Up to that time the Spirit had not been given, since Jesus had not yet been glorified.

On hearing his words, some of the people said, "Surely this man is the Prophet."

Other said, "He is the Christ."

Still others asked, "How can the Christ come from Galilee? Does not the Scripture say that the Christ will come from David's family and from Bethlehem, the town where David lived?" Thus the people were divided because of Jesus. Some wanted to seize him, but no one laid a hand on him.

Finally the temple guards went back to the chief priests and Pharisees, who asked them, "Why didn't you bring him in?"

"No one ever spoke the way this man does," the guards declared.

"You mean he had deceived you also?" the Pharisees retorted. "Has any of the rulers or of the Pharisees believed in him? No! But this mob that knows nothing of the law –there is a curse on them."

Nicodemus, who had gone to Jesus earlier and who was one of there own number, asked, "Does our law condemn anyone without first hearing him to find out what he is doing?"

They replied, "Are you from Galilee, too? Look into it, and you will find that a prophet does not come out of Galilee." Then each went to his own home.

But Jesus went to the Mount of Olives. At dawn he appeared again in the temple courts, where all the people gathered around him, and he sat down to teach them. The teachers of the law and the Pharisees brought in a woman caught in adultery. They made her stand before the group and said to Jesus, "Teacher, this woman was caught in the act of adultery. In the Law Moses commanded us to stone such women. Now what do you say?" They were using this question as a trap, in order to have a basis for accusing him.

But Jesus bent down and started to write on the ground with his finger. When they kept on questioning him, he straightened up and said to them, "If any one of you is without sin, let him be the first to throw a stone at her." Again he stooped down and wrote on the ground.

At this, those who heard began to go away one at a time, the older ones first, until only Jesus was left, with the woman still standing there. Jesus straightened up and asked her, "Woman, where are they? Has no one condemned you?"

"No one, sir," she said.

"Then neither do I condemn you," Jesus declared. "Go now and leave your life of sin."

When Jesus spoke again to the people, he said, "I am the light of the world. Whoever follows me will never walk in darkness, but will have the light of life."

The Pharisees challenged him, "Here you are, appearing as your own witness; your testimony is not valid."

Jesus answered, "Even if I testify on my own behalf, my testimony is valid, for I know where I came from and where I am going. But you have no idea where I come from or where I am going. You judge by human standards; I pass judgment on no one. But if I do judge, my decisions are right, because I am not alone. I stand with the Father, who sent me. In your own Law it is written that the testimony of two men is valid. I am one who testifies for myself; my other witness is the Father, who sent me."

Then they asked him, "Where is your father?"

"You do not know me or my Father," Jesus replied. "If you knew me, you would know my Father also." He spoke these words while teaching in the temple area near the place where the offering were put. Yet no one seized him, because his time had not yet come.

Once more Jesus said to them, "I am going away, and you will look for me, and you will die in your sin. Where I go, you cannot come."

This made the Jews ask, "Will he kill himself? Is that why he says, 'Where I go, you cannot come'?"

But he continued, "You are from below; I am from above. You are of this world; I am not of this world. I told you that you would die in your sins; if you do not believe that I am the one I claim to be, you will indeed die in your sins."

"Who are you?" they asked.

"Just what I have been claiming all along," Jesus replied. "I have much to say in judgment of you. But he who sent me is reliable, and what I have heard from him I tell the world."

They did not understand that he was telling them about his Father. So Jesus said, "When you have lifted up the Son of Man, then you will know that I am the one I claim to be and that I do nothing on my own but speak just what the Father has taught me. The one who sent me is with me; he has not left me alone, for I always do what pleases him." Even as he spoke, many put their faith in him.

To the Jews who had believed him, Jesus said, "If you hold to my teaching, you are really my disciples. Then you will know the truth and the truth will set you free."

They answered him, "We are Abraham's descendants and have never been slaves of anyone. How can you say that we shall be set free?"

Jesus replied, "I tell you the truth, everyone who sins is a slave to sin. Now a slave has not permanent place in the family, but a son belongs to it forever. So if the Son set you free, you will be free indeed. I know you are Abraham's descendants. Yet you are ready to kill me, because you have no room for my word. I am telling you what I have seen in the Father's presence, and you do what you have heard from your father."

"Abraham is our father," they answered.

"If you were Abraham's children," said Jesus, "then you would do the things Abraham did. As it is, you are determined to kill me, a man who has told you the truth that I heard from God. Abraham did not do such things. You are doing the things your own father does."

"We are not illegitimate children," they protested. "The only Father we have is God himself."

Jesus said to them, "If God were your Father, you would love me, for I came from God and now am here. I have not come on my own; but he sent me. Why is my language not clear to you? Because you are unable to hear what I say. You belong to your father, the devil, and you want to carry out your father's desire. He was a murderer from the beginning, not holding to the truth, for there is no truth in him. When he lies, he speaks his native language, for he is a liar and the father of lies. Yet because I tell the truth, you do not believe me! Can any of you prove me guilty of sin? If I am telling the truth, why don't you believe me? He who belongs to God hears what God says. The reason you do not hear is that you do not belong to God."

The Jews answered him, "Aren't we right in saying that you are a Samaritan and demon-possessed?"

"I am not possessed by a demon," said Jesus, "But I honor my Father and you dishonor me. I am not seeking glory for myself; but there is one who seeks it, and he is the judge. I tell you the truth, if anyone keeps my word, he will never see death."

At this the Jews exclaimed, "Now we know that you are demon-possessed! Abraham died and so did the prophets, yet you say that if anyone keeps your word, he will never taste death. Are you greater than our father Abraham? He died, and so did the prophets. Who do you think you are?"

Jesus replied, "If I glorify myself, my glory means nothing. My Father, whom you claim as your God, is the one who glorifies me. Though you do not know him, I know him. If I said I did not, I would be a liar like you, but I do know him and keep his word. Your father Abraham rejoiced at the thought of seeing my day; he saw it and was glad."

"You are not yet fifty years old," the Jews said to him, "and you have seen Abraham!"

"I tell you the truth," Jesus answered, "before Abraham was born, I am!" At this, they picked up stones to stone him,[4] but Jesus hid himself, slipping away from the temple grounds.

As he went along, he saw a man blind from birth. His disciples asked him, "Rabbi, who sinned, this man or his parents, that he was born blind?"

"Neither this man nor his parents sinned," said Jesus, "but this happened so that the work of God might be displayed in his life. As long as it is day, we must do the work of him who sent me. Night is coming, when no one can work. While I am in the world, I am the light of the world."

Having said this, he spit on the ground, made some mud with the saliva, and put it on the man's eyes. "Go," he told him, "wash in the Pool of Siloam" (this word means Sent). So the man went and washed, and came home seeing.

His neighbors and those who had formerly seen him begging asked, "Isn't this the same man who used to sit and beg?" Some claimed that he was.

Others said, "No, he only looks like him."

But he himself insisted, "I am the man."

"How then were your eyes opened?" they demanded.

He replied, "The man they call Jesus made some mud and put it on my eyes. He told me to go to Siloam and wash. So I went and washed, and then I could see."

"Where is this man?" they asked him.

"I don't know," he said.

They brought to the Pharisees the man who had been blind. Now the day on which Jesus had made the mud and opened the man's eyes was a Sabbath.[5] Therefore the Pharisees also asked him how he had received his sight. "He put mud on my eyes," the man replied, "and I washed, and now I see."

Some of the Pharisees said, "This man is not from God, for he does not keep the Sabbath."

But others asked, "How can a sinner do such miraculous signs?" So they were divided.

Finally they turned again to the blind man, "What have you to say about him? It was your eyes he opened."

The man replied, "He is a prophet."

The Jews still did not believe that he had been blind and had received his sight until they sent for the man's parents. "Is this your son?" they asked. "Is this the one you say was born blind? How is it that now he can see?"

"We know he is our son," the parents answered, "and we know he was born blind. But how he can see now, or who opened his eyes, we don't know. Ask him. He is of age; he will speak for himself." His parents said this because they were afraid of the Jews, for already the Jews had decided that anyone who acknowledged that Jesus was the Christ would be put out of the synagogue. That was why his parents said, "He is of age; ask him."

A second time they summoned the man who had been blind. "Give glory to God," they said. "We know this man is a sinner."

He replied, "Whether he is a sinner or not, I don't know. One thing I do know. I was blind but now I see!"

Then they asked him, "What did he do to you? How did he open your eyes?"

He answered, "I have told you already and you did not listen. Why do you want to hear it again? Do you want to become his disciples, too?"

Then they hurled insults at him and said, "You are this fellow's disciples! We are disciples of Moses! We know that God spoke to Moses, but as for this fellow, we don't even know where he comes from."

The man answered, "Now that is remarkable! You don't know where he comes from, yet he opened my eyes. We know that God does not listen to sinners. He listens to the godly man who does his will. Nobody has ever heard of opening the eyes of a man born blind. If this man were not from God, he could do nothing."

To this they replied, "You were steeped in sin at birth; how dare you lecture us!" And they threw him out.[6]

Jesus heard that they had thrown him out, and when he found him, he said, "Do you believe in the Son of Man?"

"Who is he, sir?" the man asked. "Tell me so that I may believe in him."

Jesus said, "You have now seen him; in fact, he is the one speaking with you."

Then the man said, "Lord, I believe," and he worshiped him.[7]

Jesus said, "For judgment I have come into this world, so that the blind will see and those who see will become blind."

Some Pharisees who were with him heard him say this and asked. "What? Are we blind too?"

Jesus said, "If you were blind, you would not be guilty of sin; but now that you claim you can see, your guilt remains."

I tell you the truth, the man who does you enter the sheep pen by the gate, but climbs in by some other way, is a thief and a robber. The man who enters by the gate is the shepherd of his sheep. The watchman opens the gate for him, and the sheep listens to his voice. He calls his own sheep by name and leads them out. When he has brought out all his own, he goes on ahead of them, and his sheep follow him because they know his voice. But they will never follow a stranger; in fact, they will run away from him because they do not recognize a stranger's voice." Jesus used this figure of speech, but they did not understand what he was telling them.

Therefore Jesus said again, "I tell you the truth, I am the gate for the sheep. All who ever came before me were thieves and robbers, but the sheep did not listen to them. I am the gate; whoever enters through me will be saved. He will come in and go out, and find pasture. The thief comes only to steal and kill and destroy; I have come that they may have life, and have it to the full.

"I am the good shepherd. The good shepherd lays down his life for the sheep. The hired hand is not the shepherd who owns the sheep. So when he sees the wolf coming, he abandons the sheep and runs away. Then the wolf attacks the flock and scatters it. The man runs away because he is a hired hand and cares nothing for the sheep.

"I am the good shepherd; I know my sheep and my sheep know me – just as the Father knows me and I know the Father – and I lay down my life for the sheep. I have other sheep that are not of this sheep pen. I must bring them also. They too will listen to my voice, and there shall be one flock and one shepherd. The reason my Father loves me is that I lay down my life – only to take it up again. No one takes it from me, but I lay it down of my own accord. I have authority to lay it down and authority to take it up again. This command I received from my Father."

At these words the Jews were again divided. Many of them said, "He is demon-possessed and raving mad. Why listen to him?"

But others said, "These are not the sayings of a man possessed by a demon. Can a demon open the eyes of the blind?"

Then came the Feast of Dedication at Jerusalem. (*Nov/Dec*) It was winter, and Jesus was in the temple area walking in Solomon's colonnade. The Jews gathered around him, saying, "How long will you keep us in suspense? If you are the Christ, tell us plainly."

Jesus answered, "I did tell you, but you do not believe. The miracles I do in my Father's name speak for me, but you do not believe because you are not my sheep. My sheep listen to my voice; I know them, and they follow me. I give them eternal life, and they shall never perish; no one can snatch them out of my hand. My Father who has given them to me, is greater than all, no one can snatch them out of my Father's hand. I and the Father are one."

Again the Jews picked up stones to stone him,[8] but Jesus said to them, "I have shown you many great miracles from the Father. For which of these do you stone me?"

"We are not stoning you for any of these," replied the Jews, "but for blasphemy, because you, a mere man, claim to be God."

Jesus answered them, "Is it not written in your Law, 'I have said you are gods'? If he called them 'gods,' to whom the word of God came – and the Scripture cannot be broken– what about the one whom the Father set apart as his very own and sent into the world? Why then do you accuse me of blasphemy because I said, 'I am God's Son'? Do not believe me unless I do what my Father does. But if I do it, even though you do not believe me, believe the miracles, that you may know and understand that the Father is in me, and I in the Father."

Again they tried to seize him, but he escaped their grasp.

Then Jesus went back across the Jordan to the place where John had been baptizing in the early days. Here he stayed and many people came to him. They said, "Though John never performed a miraculous sign, all that John said about this man was true." And in that place many believed in Jesus.

Now a man named Lazarus was sick. He was from Bethany, the village of Mary and her sister Martha. This Mary, whose brother Lazarus now lay sick, was the same one who poured perfume on the Lord and wiped his feet with her hair. So the sisters sent word to Jesus, "Lord, the one you love is sick."

When he heard this, Jesus said, "This sickness will not end in death. No, it is for God's glory so that God's Son may be glorified through it." Jesus loved Martha and her sister and Lazarus. Yet when he heard that Lazarus was sick, he stayed where he was two more days.

Then he said to his disciples, "Let us go back to Judea."

"But Rabbi," they said, "a short while ago the Jews tried to stone you, and yet you are going back there?"

Jesus answered, "Are there not twelve hours of daylight? A man who walks by day will not stumble, for he sees by this world's light. It is when he walks by night that he stumbles, for he has no light."

After he had said this, he went on to tell them, "Our friend Lazarus has fallen asleep; but I am going there to wake him up."

His disciples replied, "Lord, if he sleeps, he will get better." Jesus had been speaking of his death, but his disciples thought he meant natural sleep.

So then he told them plainly, "Lazarus is dead, and for your sake I am glad I was not there, so that you may believe. But let us go to him."

Then Thomas (called Didymus) said to the rest of the disciples, "Let us also go, that we may die with him."

On his arrival, Jesus found that Lazarus had already been in the tomb for four days. Bethany was less than two miles from Jerusalem, and many Jews had come to Martha and Mary to comfort them in the loss of their brother. When Martha heard that Jesus was coming, she went out to meet him, but Mary stayed at home.

"Lord," Martha said to Jesus, "if you had been here, my brother would not have died. But I know that even now God will give you whatever you ask."

Jesus said to her, "Your brother will rise again."

Martha answered, "I know he will rise again in the resurrection at the last day."

Jesus said to her, "I am the resurrection and the life. He who believes in me will live, even though he dies; and whoever lives and believes in me will never die. Do you believe this?"

"Yes, Lord," she told him, "I believe that you are the Christ, the Son of God, who was to come into the world."

And after she had said this, she went back and called her sister Mary aside. "The Teacher is here," she said, "and is asking for you."

When Mary heard this, she got up quickly and went to him. Now Jesus had not yet entered the village, but was still at the place where Martha had met him. When the Jews who had been with Mary in the house, comforting her, noticed how quickly she got up and went out, they followed her, supposing she was going to the tomb to mourn there. When Mary reached the place where Jesus was and saw him, she fell at his feet and said, "Lord, if you had been here, my brother would not have died."

When Jesus saw her weeping, and the Jews who had come along with her also weeping, he was deeply moved in spirit and troubled.

"Where have you laid him?" he asked.

"Come and see, Lord," they replied.

Jesus wept.

Then the Jews said, "See how he loved him!"

But some of them said, "Could not he who opened the eyes of the blind man have kept this man from dying?"

Jesus, once more deeply moved, came to the tomb. It was a cave with a stone laid across the entrance. "Take away the stone," he said.

"But, Lord," said Martha, the sister of the dead man, "by this time there is a bad odor, for he had been there four days."

Then Jesus said, "Did I not tell you that if you believed, you would see the glory of God?"

So they took away the stone. Then Jesus looked up and said, "Father, I thank you that you have heard me. I knew that you always hear me, but I said this for the benefit of the people standing here, that they may believe that you sent me."

When he had said this, Jesus called in a loud voice, "Lazarus, come out!" The dead man came out, his hands and feet wrapped with strips of linen, and a cloth around his face.

Jesus said to them, "Take off the grave clothes and let him go."

Therefore many of the Jews who had come to visit Mary, and had seen what Jesus did, put their faith in him. But some of them went to the Pharisees and told them what Jesus had done. Then the chief priests and the Pharisees called a meeting of the Sanhedrin.

"What are we accomplishing?" they asked. "Here is this man performing many miraculous signs. If we let him go on like this, everyone will believe in him, and then the Romans will come and take away both our place and our nation."

Then one of them, named Caiaphas, who was high priest that year, spoke up, "You know nothing at all! You do not realize that it is better for you that one man die for the people than that the whole nation perish."

He did not say this on his own, but as high priest that year he prophesied that Jesus would die for the Jewish nation, and not only for that nation but also for the scattered children of God, to bring them together and make them one. So from that day on they plotted to take his life.

Therefore Jesus no longer moved about publicly among the Jews. Instead he withdrew to a region near the desert, to a village called Ephraim,[9] where he stayed with his disciples.

STUDY NOTES

1. Six months after His journey to Jerusalem for third Passover feast, Jesus is traveling to Jerusalem again- this time for the Feast of Tabernacles.[See Chapter 22 Study Note No 1]. Jesus is undertaking this journey after He had foretold four times about the suffering, death and resurrection, which He was to undergo in Jerusalem. Yet those were not going to take place in this particular journey. They happen only in His next journey to Jerusalem, which is going to be six months later- when He goes there for the next Passover feast.

All the four gospel writers begin to tell us almost in unison about a journey Jesus made from Galilee to Jerusalem (Mt. 18:35 and 19:1 / Mk. 9:50 and 10:1/ Lk. 9:50,51 / Jn. 7:1-10). But all of them are not talking of one and the same journey. While John describes Jesus' travel for the Feast of Tabernacles, Matthew, Mark and Luke describe Jesus' travel from Galilee to Jerusalem to celebrate the fourth Passover Feast- six months after the Feast of Tabernacles, which incidentally was His last journey.

2. Here we see that even the public knew that the leaders were plotting to kill Jesus!

3. None of their attempts were fruitful because the appointed time had not come. John continues to give us the details of the aborted attempt they had just made.

4. This is the third unsuccessful attempt on the life of Jesus. Notably this attempt is made on a Sabbath day! The other unsuccessful bids made on His life are as follows:

First unsuccessful attempt Chapter 3 Study Note No: 2

Second unsuccessful attempt Chapter 13 Study Note No: 1

Fourth unsuccessful attempt Chapter 19 Study Note No: 8

5. Since this happened on the same day that the Jews tried stone Jesus, we know that the attempt to murder Him was made on a Sabbath day.

6. They throw him out because he proclaimed that Jesus came from God.

7. He is exactly the opposite of the one who betrayed Jesus after being miraculously healed by Him in Chapter 7 Study Note No: 2.

8. This is the fourth and last unsuccessful attempt to murder Jesus.

First unsuccessful attempt Chapter 3 Study Note No: 2

Second unsuccessful attempt Chapter 13 Study Note No: 1

Third unsuccessful attempt Chapter 19 Study Note No: 4

9. Though there are no details of His return to Galilee from Ehraim, since Jesus begins His last journey to Jerusalem from Galilee, it is understood that He had returned to Galilee after a brief stay here.

XX

JOURNEY FROM GALILEE TO JERUSALEM FOR THE LAST TIME

[*After his return from Ephraim....*]
(Lk. 9:51-56)

As the time approached for him to be taken up to heaven, Jesus resolutely set out for Jerusalem.[1] And he sent messengers on ahead, who went into a Samaritan village to get things ready for him; but the people there did not welcome him, because he was heading for Jerusalem When the disciples James and John saw this, they asked, "Lord, do you want us to call fire down from heaven to destroy them even as Elijah did?" But Jesus turned and rebuked them, and he said, "You do not know what kind of spirit you are of, for the Son of Man did not came to destroy men's lives, but to save them." And they went to another village.

(Mt. 11:20-30 / Lk. 10:1-37)

After this the Lord appointed seventy other and sent them two by two ahead of him to every town and place where he was about to go. He told them[2], "The harvest is plentiful, but the workers are few. Ask the Lord of the harvest, therefore, to send out workers into his harvest field. Go! I am sending you out like lambs among wolves. Do not take a purse or bag or sandals, and do not greet anyone on the road.

"When you enter a house, first say, 'Peace to this house.' If a man of peace is there, your peace will rest on him; if not, it will return to you. Stay in that house, eating and drinking whatever they give you, for the worker deserves his wages. Do not move around from house to house.

"When you enter a town and are welcomed, eat what is set before you. Heal the sick who are there and tell them, 'The kingdom of God is near you.' But when you enter a town and are not welcomed, go into its streets and say, 'Even the dust of your town that sticks to our feet we wipe off against you. Yet be sure of this: The kingdom of God is near.' I tell you, it will be more bearable on that day for Sodom than for that town.

Then Jesus began to denounce the cities in which most of his miracles had been performed, because they did not repent.[3]

"Woe to you, Korazin! Woe to you, Bethsaida! For if the miracles that were performed in you had been performed in Tyre and Sidon,[4] they would have repented long ago, sitting in sackcloth and ashes. But it will be more bearable for Tyre and Sidon at the judgment than for you. And you, Capernaum, will you be lifted up to the skies? No, you will go down to the depths. If the miracles that were performed in you had been performed in Sodom it would have remained to this day. But I tell you it will be more bearable for Sodom on the Day of Judgment than for you.

"He who listens to you listens to me; he who rejects you rejects me; but he who rejects me rejects him who sent me."

"The seventy-two returned[5] with joy and said, "Lord, even the demons submit to us in you name."

He replied, "I saw Satan fall like lightning from heaven. I have given you authority to trample on snakes and scorpions and to overcome all the power of the enemy; nothing will harm you. However, do not rejoice that the spirits submit to you, but rejoice that your names are written in heaven."

At that time Jesus, full of joy through the Holy Spirit, said, "I praise you, Father, Lord of heaven and earth, because you have hidden these things from the wise and learned, and revealed them to little children. Yes, Father, for this was your good pleasure.

"All things have been committed to me by my Father. No one knows who the Son is except the Father, and not one knows who the Father is except the Son and those to whom the Son chooses to reveal him.

"Come to me, all you who are weary and burdened, and I will give your rest. Take my yoke upon you and learn from me, for I am gentle and humble in heart, and you will find rest for your souls. For my yoke is easy and my burden is light."

Then he turned to his disciples and said privately, "Blessed are the eyes that see what you see. For I tell you that many prophets and kings wanted to see what you see but did not see it, and to hear what you hear but did not hear it."

On one occasion an expert in the law stood up to test Jesus. "Teacher,' he asked, "What must I do to inherit eternal life?"

"What is written in the Law?" he replied. "How do you read it?"

He answered: " 'Love the Lord your God with all your heart and with all your soul and with all your strength and with all your mind; and, 'Love your neighbor as yourself.' "

"You have answered correctly," Jesus replied. "Do this and you will live."

But he wanted to justify himself, so he asked Jesus, "And who is my neighbor?"

In reply Jesus said: "A man was going down from Jerusalem to Jericho, when he fell into the hands of robbers. They stripped him of his clothes, beat him and went away, leaving him half dead. A priest happened to be going down the same road, and when he saw the man, he passed by on the other side. So too, a Levite, when he came to the place and saw him, passed by on the other side. But a Samaritan, as he traveled, came where the man was; and when he saw him, he took pity on him. He went to him and bandaged his wounds, pouring on oil and wine. Then he put the man on his own donkey, took him to an inn and took care of him. The next day he took out two silver coins and gave them to the innkeeper. 'Look after him,' he said, 'and when I return, I will reimburse you for any extra expense you may have.'

"Which of these three do you think was a neighbor to the man who fell into the hands of robbers?"

The expert in the law replied, "The one who had mercy on him."

Jesus told him, "Go and do likewise."

(Mt. 19:1,2 / Mk. 10:1)

Jesus then left that place and went into the region of Judea and across the Jordan. Again large crowds of people came to him, and as was his custom, he taught them and healed them there.

(Mt. 19:3-15 / Mk. 10:2-16 / Lk. 16:18, 18:1-17)

Then Jesus told his disciples a parable to show them that they should always pray and not give up. He said: "In a certain town there was a judge who neither feared God nor cared about men. And there was a widow in that town who kept coming to him with the plea, 'Grand me justice against my adversary.'

"For some time he refused. But finally he said to himself, 'Even though I don't fear God or care about men, yet because this widow keeps bothering me, I will see that she gets justice, so that she won't eventually wear me out with her coming!' "

And the Lord said, "Listen to what the unjust judge says. And will not God bring about justice for his chosen ones, who cry out to him day and night? Will he keep putting them off? I tell you, he will see that they get justice, and quickly. However, when the Son of Man comes, will he find faith on the earth?"

To some who were confident of their own righteousness and looked down on everybody else, Jesus told this parable: "Two men went up to the temples to pray, one a Pharisee and the other a tax collector. The Pharisee stood up and prayed about himself: 'God, I thank you that I am not like other men – robbers, evildoers, adulterers – or even like this tax collector. I fast twice a week and give a tenth of all I get.'

"But the tax collector stood at a distance. He would not even look up to heaven, but beat his breast and said, 'God, have mercy on me, a sinner.'

"I tell you that this man, rather than the other, went home justified before God. For everyone who exalts himself will be humbled, and he who humbles himself will be exalted."

Some Pharisees came and tested him by asking, "Is it lawful for a man to divorce his wife for any and every reason?"

"What did Moses command you?" he replied. They said, "Moses permitted a man to write a certificate of divorce and send her away."

"It was because your hearts were hard that Moses wrote you this law, "Jesus replied. "But it was not this way from the beginning: At the beginning of creation God 'made them male and female.' 'For this reason a man will leave his father and mother and be united to his wife, and the two will become one flesh." So they are no longer two, but one. Therefore what God had joined together, let man not separate."

When they were in the house again, the disciples asked Jesus about this. He answered, "Any one who divorces his wife, except for marital unfaithfulness and marries another woman commits adultery against her. And if she divorces her husband and marries another man, she commits adultery."

The disciples said to him, "If this is the situation between a husband and wife, it is better not to marry."

Jesus replied, "Not everyone can accept this word, but only those to whom it has been given. For some are eunuchs because they were born that way; others were made that way by men; and others have made themselves eunuchs because of the kingdom of heaven. The one who can accept this should accept it."

Then little children were brought to Jesus for him to place his hands on them and pray for them. But when the disciples saw this, they rebuked those who brought them.

When Jesus saw this, he was indignant. Jesus called the children to him and said, "Let the little children come to me, and do not hinder them, for the kingdom of God belongs to such as these. I tell you the truth, anyone who will not receive the kingdom of God like a little child will never enter it." And he took the children in his arms, put his hands on them and blessed them.

STUDY NOTES

1. Now Jesus is traveling from Galilee to Judea to attend the fourth and the final Passover Feast in His earthly ministry. Matthew, Mark and Luke tell us about this last journey in the following passages in their respective gospels:

i) Mt. 19:1 – He left Galilee and went into the region of Judea to the other side of the Jordan.

ii) Mt. 20:17 – As Jesus was going up to Jerusalem.

iii) Mt. 20:29 – As Jesus and his disciples were leaving Jericho.

iv) Mk. 10:1 – Went into the region of Judea and across the Jordan.

v) Mk. 10:32 – They were on their way up to Jerusalem, with Jesus leading the way.

vi) Lk. 9:51 – Jesus resolutely set out for Jerusalem.

vii) Lk. 19:1 – Jesus entered Jericho and was passing through.

viii) Lk. 19:28 – He went on ahead, going up to Jerusalem. Though Luke begins to describe this last journey in 9:51, he inserts many incidents from the other travels in this journey. A few examples are as follows:

i) Lk. 10:38 – As Jesus and his disciples were on their way...

ii) Lk. 13:22 – As he made his way to Jerusalem...

iii) Lk. 14:25 – Large crowds were traveling with Jesus...

iv) Lk. 17:11 – Now on his way to Jerusalem...

It is to be noted that Jesus did not travel through Samaria in this last journey. It is an obvious fact that He instead took the route via the other side of Jordan. (Mt. 19:1 / Mk. 10:1) But in the above-quoted passages we can find that Luke had included an incident that took place while Jesus traveled through Samaria (Lk. 17:11)!

2. These instructions are similar to the ones Jesus had given earlier while sending out his disciples. See Chapter 15 Study Note No: 2.

3. These cities had witnessed a good portion of Jesus' three and half year's ministry and yet did not respond positively. Therefore on His final departure, Jesus rebukes them. This is virtually His farewell speech- given with a heavy heart.

4. Jesus compares them with gentile cities.

5. Jesus must have stayed back in the village itself after He had sent out the seventy disciples for ministry. Now after completing their ministry they come back to Him.

XXI
TO JERUSALEM THROUGH JERICHO

(Mt. 19:16-20:28 / Mk. 10:17-45 / Lk. 18:18-34,19:28)

As Jesus started on his way, a certain ruler ran up to him and fell on his knees before him. "Good teacher," he asked, "what good thing must I do to inherit eternal life?"

"Why do you call me good?" Jesus answered. "No one is good - except God alone. If you want to enter life, obey the commandments."

"Which ones?" the man inquired.

Jesus replied, " You know the commandments 'Do not murder, do not commit adultery, do not steal, do not give false testimony, do not defraud, honor your father and mother,' and 'love your neighbor as yourself.' "

"All these I have kept since I was a boy," the young man said. "What do I still lack?"

Jesus looked at him and loved him. "You still lack one thing. If you want to be perfect, go, sell your possessions and give to the poor, and you will have treasure in heaven. Then come, follow me."

When the young man heard this his face fell and he went away sad, because he had great wealth.

Jesus looked around and said to his disciples, "How hard it is for the rich to enter the kingdom of God!"

The disciples were amazed at his words. But Jesus said again, "Children, how hard it is for those who trust in riches to enter the kingdom of God! It is easier for a camel to go through the eye of a needle than for a rich man to enter the kingdom of God."

The disciples were even more amazed, and said to each other, "Who then can be saved?"

Jesus looked at them and said, "With man this is impossible, but not with God; all things are possible with God."

Peter answered him, "We have left everything to follow you! What then will there be for us?"

Jesus said to them, "I tell you the truth, at the renewal of all things, when the Son of Man sits on his glorious throne, you who have followed me will also sit on twelve thrones, judging the twelve tribes of Israel.

"I tell you the truth," Jesus replied, "no one who has left home or wife or brothers or sisters or mother or father or children or fields for me and the gospel will fail to receive a hundred times as much in this present age (homes, brother, sisters, mothers, children and fields – and with them, persecutions) and in the age to come, eternal life. But many who are first will be last, and the last first."

"For the kingdom of heaven is like a landowner who went out early in the morning to hire men to work in his vineyard. He agreed to pay them a denarius for the day and sent them into his vineyard.

"About the third hour he went out and saw others standing in the marketplace doing nothing. He told them, 'You also go and work in my vineyard, and I will pay you whatever is right.' So they went.

"He went out again about the sixth hour and the ninth hour and did the same thing. About the eleventh hour he went out and found still others standing around. He asked them, 'Why have you been standing here all day long doing nothing?'

" 'Because no one has hired us,' they answered.

"He said to them, 'You also go and work in my vineyard.'

"When evening came, the owner of the vineyard said to his foreman, 'Call the workers and pay them their wages, beginning with the last ones hired and going on to the first.'

"The workers who were hired about the eleventh hour came and each received a denarius. So when those came who were hired first, they expected to receive more. But each one of them also received a denarius. When they received it, they began to grumble against the landowner. 'These men who were hired last worked only one hour,' they said, 'and you have made them equal to us who have borne the burden of the work and the heat of the day.'

"But he answered one of them, 'Friend, I am not being unfair to you. Didn't you agree to work for a denarius? Take your pay and go. I want to give the man who was hired last the same as I gave you. Don't I have the right to do what I want with my own money? Or are you envious because I am generous?'

"So the last will be first, and the first will be last."

They were on their way up to Jerusalem, with Jesus leading the way, and the disciples were astonished, while those who followed were afraid. He took the Twelve disciples aside and told them what was going to happen to him. "We are going up to Jerusalem, and everything that is written by the prophets about the Son of Man will be fulfilled. The Son of Man will be betrayed to the chief priests and teachers of the law. They will condemn him to death and will hand him over to the Gentiles, who will mock him and spit on him, flog him and kill him. Three days later he will rise."[1]

The disciples did not understand any of this. Its meaning was hidden from them, and they did not know what he was talking about.

Then the mother of Zebedee's sons came to Jesus with her sons and, kneeling down, asked a favor of him.[2]

"What is it you want?" he asked.

She said, "Grant that one of these two sons of mine may sit at your right and the other at your left in your kingdom."

"You don't know what you are asking," Jesus said to them. "Can you drink the cup I am going to drink?"

"We can," they answered.

"Jesus said to them, "You will indeed drink from my cup, but to sit at my right or left is not for me to grant. These places belong to those for whom they have been prepared by my Father."

When the ten heard about this, they were indignant with James and John. Jesus called them together and said, "You know that those who are regarded as rulers of the Gentiles lord it over them and their high officials exercise authority over them. Not so with you. Instead, whoever wants to become great among you must be your servant, and whoever wants to be first must be slave of all. For even the Son of Man did not come to be served, but to serve, and to give his life as a ransom for many."

(Lk. 19:1-10)

Jesus entered Jericho and was passing through. A man was there by the name of Zacchaeus; he was a chief tax collector and was wealthy. He wanted to see who Jesus was, but being a short man he could not, because of the crowd. So he ran ahead and climbed a sycamore fig tree to see him, since Jesus was coming that way.

When Jesus reached the spot, he looked up and said to him, "Zacchaeus, come down immediately. I must stay at your house today." So he came down at once and welcomed him gladly.

All the people saw this and began to mutter, "He has gone to be the guest of a 'sinner'".

But Zacchaeus stood up and said to the Lord, "Look, Lord! Here and now I give half of my possessions to the poor, and if I have cheated anybody out of anything. I will pay back four times the amount."

Jesus said to him, "Today salvation has come to this house, because this man, too, is a son of Abraham. For the Son of Man came to seek and to save what was lost."

(Mt. 20:29-34 / Mk. 10:46-52 / Lk. 18:35-43)

As Jesus and his disciples were leaving Jericho,[3] a large crowd followed him. Two blind men (*Bartimaeus that is, the Son of Timaeus* was one of them) were sitting by the roadside.[4]

When they heard the crowd going by, asked what was happening. They told them, "Jesus of Nazareth is passing by."

They called out, "Jesus, Son of David, have mercy on us!" Those who led the way rebuked him and told him to be quiet, but he shouted all the more, "Son of David, have mercy on us!"

Jesus stopped and called them.

So they called to the blind men, "Cheer up! On your feet! He's calling you." Throwing his cloak aside, he (*Bartimaeus*) jumped to his feet and came to Jesus.

"What do you want me to do for you?" Jesus asked.

"Lord," they answered, "we want our sight."

"Go," said Jesus, "Your faith has healed you." Immediately they received their sight and followed Jesus along the road praising God. When all the people saw it, they also praised God.

STUDY NOTES

1. This is the fifth time Jesus is foretelling His suffering His death and resurrection. Although Jesus had previously talked about it four times – six months ago, we can find that there is a marked difference between those and this present one. Unlike the previous occasions, this time we

find Jesus specially mentioning that 'these things are going to happen in this journey'. ("We are going up to Jerusalem, and everything that is written by the prophets about the Son of Man will be fulfilled")

2. John despite being an eyewitness to this incidence fails to mention this in his gospel. Where as all the other three gospel writers mention it! Other similar occasions are:

Chapter 18 Study Note No: 3

Chapter 25 Study Note No: 4

3. Even though Luke says that this happened before Jesus entered Jericho, since all the other gospel writers say that this happened only after they left Jericho, we concur with the latter.

4. Matthew states that there were two blind men. At the same time, Mark and Luke state that there was one blind man. Therefore we presume that there were actually two blind men involved in the incident– Matthew talks about both of them, Mark and Luke give details about one of them. Chapter 12 Study Note No: 2 gives another such incident

THE FINAL WEEK OF JESUS CHRIST

XXII

SIX DAYS BEFORE THE PASSOVER (SATURDAY - THE SABBATH DAY)

1.	Saturday (Sabbath day)	Six days before the Passover, Jesus arrived at Bethany.(Jn. 12:1)
2.	Sunday	Jesus enters Jerusalem riding on a colt. (Mt. 11:1-11)
3.	Monday	Jesus curses the fig tree on the way to Jerusalem. (Mk. 11:12-26)
4.	Tuesday	The chief priests and others question the authority of Jesus. Jesus' reply to this is followed by a Sermon that continues to the mount of olives. (Mk. 11:27-13:37)
5.	Wednesday	Jesus takes part in a feast in the house of Simon the leper and there Mary Magdalene pours expensive perfume on Him. At the same time a plot to kill Jesus is discussed in the house of the chief priest. It was on this day that Judas agreed to betray Jesus. (Mk. 14:1-11)
6.	Thursday (Passover feast)	After the Passover feast in Jerusalem, Jesus is arrested in Gethsemane. (Mk. 14:12-53)
7.	Friday	Jesus is crucified in the morning and laid to rest in the evening. (Mk. 15:21-47)
8.	Saturday (Sabbath day)	(Lk. 23:56)
9.	Sunday	Resurrection of Jesus (Mk. 16:1-11)

The table giving the events of the holy week[1]

(Jn. 11:55-12:1 & 9-11)

When it was almost time for the Jewish Passover, men went up from the country to Jerusalem for their ceremonial cleansing before the Passover. They kept looking for Jesus,[2] and as they stood in the temple area they asked one another, "What do you think? Isn't he coming to the Feast at all?"[*By this time Jesus must be somewhere near Jerusalem*] But the chief priests and Pharisees had given orders that if anyone found out where Jesus was, he should report it so that they might arrest him.

Day:1 SATURDAY:

Six days before the Passover, Jesus arrived at Bethany, where Lazarus lived, whom Jesus had raised from the dead.

Meanwhile, a large crowd of Jews found out that Jesus was there and came, not only because of him but also to see Lazarus, whom he had raised from the dead.[3] So the chief priests made plans to kill Lazarus as well, for on account of him many of the Jews were going over to Jesus and putting their faith in him.

STUDY NOTES

1. To get the chronological sequence of the holy week, I have gone by the gospel of Mark. It is because the writer of the gospel of Mark has given more importance than the others for the chronological sequence in general and the holy week in particular where he gives the day by day account of the week.

When tabulated as per Mark's gospel, the following interesting facts come to light:

i) Although Matthew and Luke give an impression that the cleansing of the temple was done on the day of Jesus' triumphant entry, it is not so.

ii) Matthew gives an impression that the withered fig tree was noticed on the same day. Actually it was noticed only on the next day.

2. The public is anxious to know if Jesus will visit Jerusalem at all in this hostile atmosphere. Even during the feast of tabernacles, six months ago, they had waited for His arrival in Jerusalem with a similar feeling. See Chapter 19.

This is the fourth and the last Passover Feast.

First Passover Feast Chapter 4 Study Note No: 1

Second Passover Feast Chapter 8 Study Note No: 1

Third Passover Feast Chapter 16 Study Note No: 3

3. Jesus resurrected Lazarus from the dead six months ago during His last visit. The plot to murder Jesus gathered momentum only after this miracle. That was why Jesus stayed in Ephraim and returned to Galilee from there itself. Since Jesus is coming back only now after that miracle people are eager to have a look at the performer of that miracle and they gather in strength to see Him. As a result the people who plotted to kill Jesus now wanted to kill Lazarus also!

XXIII
THE NEXT DAY (SUNDAY)

Day: 2 SUNDAY:

(Mt. 21:1-11/Mk. 11:1-11/Lk. 19:29-44/Jn. 12:12-19)

The next day, as they approached Jerusalem and came to Bethphage on the Mount of Olives, Jesus sent two disciples, saying to them, "Go to the village ahead of you, and at once you will find a donkey tied there, with her colt by her, which no one has ever ridden. Untie them and bring them to me. If anyone asks you 'Why are you untying it?' tell him, 'The Lord needs them.' and he will send them right away."

This took place to fulfill what was spoken through the prophet:

"Say to the Daughter of Zion,

'See, your king comes to you,

gentle and riding on a donkey,

on a colt, the foal of a donkey.' "

At first his disciples did not understand all this. Only after Jesus was glorified did they realize that these things had been written about him and that they had done these things to him.

Those who were sent ahead went and found a colt outside in the street, tied at a doorway. As they were untying the colt, its owners standing there asked them, "Why are you untying the colt?" They answered, "The Lord needs them" as Jesus had told them to, and the people let them go. They brought the donkey and the colt to Jesus and threw their cloaks over it [*the colt*], he sat on it.

The great crowd that had come for the Feast heard that Jesus was on his way to Jerusalem. They took palm branches and went out to meet him, shouting,

"Hosanna! Blessed is he who comes in the name of the Lord! Blessed is the King of Israel!"

A very large crowd spread their cloaks on the road, while others cut branches from the trees and spread them on the road.

When he came near the place where the road goes down the Mount of Olives, the whole crowd of disciples began joyfully to praise God in loud voices for all the miracles they had seen, the crowds that went ahead of him and those that followed him shouted,

"Hosanna to the Son of David!"

"Blessed is the king who comes in the name of the Lord!"

"Blessed is the coming kingdom of our father David! Hosanna in the highest! Peace in heaven and glory in the highest!" [*The leaders expected the people report to them if they even knew Jesus' whereabouts!*]

Some of the Pharisees in the crowd said to Jesus, "Teacher, rebuke your disciples!"

"I tell you," he replied, "if they keep quiet, the stones will cry out."

As they approached Jerusalem and saw the city, he wept over it and said, "If you, even you, had only known on this day what would bring you peace – but now it is hidden from your eyes. The days will come upon you when your enemies will build and embankment against you and encircle you and hem you in on every side. They will dash you to the round, you and the children within your walls. They will not leave one stone on another, because you did not recognize the time of God's coming to you."

When Jesus entered Jerusalem, the whole city was stirred and asked, "Who is this?"

The crowds answered, "This is Jesus, the prophet from Nazareth in Galilee."

Now the crowd that was with him when he called Lazarus from the tomb and raised him from the dead continued to spread the word. Many people, because they had heard that he had given this miraculous sign, went out to meet him. So the Pharisees said to one another, "See, this is getting us nowhere. Look how the whole world has gone after him!"

Jesus went to the temple. He looked around at everything, but since it was already late, he went out to Bethany with the Twelve.

XXIV
THE CLEANSING OF TEMPLE (MONDAY)

Day: 3 MONDAY:
(Mt. 21:12-19/Mk. 11:12-19/Lk. 19:45,46/Jn. 2: 13-17)
The next day as they were leaving Bethany, Jesus was hungry. Seeing in the distance a fig tree in leaf, he went to find out if it had any fruit. When he reached it, he found nothing but leaves, because it was not the season for figs. Then he said to the tree, "May no one ever eat fruit from you again." And his disciples heard him say it. On reaching Jerusalem, Jesus entered the temple area and in the temple courts he found men selling cattle, sheep and doves, and others sitting at tables exchanging money. So he made a whip out of cords, and drove out all who were buying and selling there. He scattered the coins of the moneychangers and overturned their tables and the benches of those selling doves and would not allow anyone to carry merchandise through the temple courts. "Is it not written;" he said to them,

" 'My house will be called

a house of prayer for all nations'?

But you have made it a den of robbers.' "

His disciples remembered that it is written: "Zeal for your house will consume me."

The blind and the lame came to him at the temple, and he healed them. But when the chief priests and the teachers of the law saw the wonderful things he did and the children shouting in the temple area, "Hosanna to the Son of David," they were indignant.

"Do you hear what these children are saying?" they asked him.

"Yes," replied Jesus, "have you never read,

"From the lips of children and infants

you have ordained praise'?"

The chief priests and the teachers of the law heard this and began looking for a way to kill him, for they feared him,[1] because the whole crowd was amazed at his teaching. When evening came, he left them and went out of the city to Bethany, where he spent the night.

STUDY NOTES

1. On the day when Jesus cleansed the temple neither did the Pharisees and the High priests try to stop Him nor challenge His authority. Instead they were looking for a way to kill Him!

XXV
LAST SERMON OF JESUS IN THE TEMPLE (TUESDAY)

Day: 4 TUESDAY:

(Mt. 21:20-22/Mk. 11:20-26)

In the morning, as they went along, they saw the fig tree withered from the roots.[1] Peter remembered and said to Jesus, "Rabbi, look! The fig tree you cursed has withered!"

Jesus replied, "I tell you the truth, if you have faith and do not doubt, not only can you do what was done to the fig tree, but also you can say to this mountain, 'Go, throw yourself into the sea,' and does not doubt in his heart but believes that what he says will happen, it will be done for him. Therefore I tell you, whatever you ask for in prayer, believe that you have received it, and it will be yours. And when you stand praying,[2] if you hold anything against anyone, forgive him, so that your Father in heaven may forgive you your sins. But if you do not forgive neither will your father who is in heaven forgive your sins."

(Mt. 21:23-27/Mk. 11:27-33/Lk. 20:1-8/Jn. 2:18-22)

They arrived again in Jerusalem, and while Jesus was walking and teaching in the temple courts, the chief priests, the teachers of the law and the elders came to him. "Tell us, by what authority are you doing these things?" they asked. "And who gave you authority to do this?"

Jesus replied, "I will also ask you one question. If you answer me, I will tell you by what authority I am doing these things. John's baptism – where did it come from? Was it from heaven, or from men?"

They discussed it among themselves and said, "If we say, 'From heaven,' he will ask, 'then why didn't you believe him?' But if we say, 'From men' – we are afraid of the people. All the people will stone us, because they are persuaded that John was a prophet."

So they answered Jesus, "We don't know where it was from." Then he said, "Neither will I tell you by what authority I am doing these things."

Then the Jews had demanded of him, "What miraculous sign can you show us to prove your authority to do all this?"

Jesus answered them, "Destroy this temple, and I will raise it again in three days."

The Jews replied, "It taken forty-six years to build this temple, and you are going to raise it in three days?" But the temple he had spoken of was his body. After he was raised from the dead, his disciples recalled what he has said. Then they believed the Scripture and the words that Jesus had spoken.

(Mt. 21:28-32)

"What do you think? There was a man who had two sons. He went to the first and said, 'Son, go and work today in the vineyard.'

"'I will not,' he answered, but later he changed his mind and went.

"Then the father went to the other son and said the same thing. He answered, 'I will, sir,' but he did not go.

"Which of the two did what his father wanted?"

"The first," they answered.

Jesus said to them, "I tell you the truth, the tax collectors and the prostitutes are entering the kingdom of God ahead of you. For John came to you to show you the way of righteousness, and you did not believe him, but the tax collectors and the prostitutes did. And even after you saw this, you did not repent and believe him.[3]"

(Mt. 21:33-46/Mk. 12:1-12/Lk. 20: 9-19)

He went on to tell the people this parable: "A man planted a vineyard, he put a wall around it, dug a pit for the winepress and built a watchtower. Then he rented vineyard to some farmers and went away for a long time on a journey. At harvest time he sent a servant to the tenants to collect from them some of the fruit of the vineyard. But they seized him, beat him and sent him away empty-handed. Then he sent another servant to them; they struck this man on the head and treated him shamefully.

"He sent still a third, and they wounded him and threw him out. He sent still another, and that one they killed. He sent other servants to them, more than the first time; some of them they beat, others they killed.

"Then the owner of the vineyard said, 'what shall I do? I will send my son, whom I love, perhaps they will respect him.'

"But when the tenants saw him, they talked the matter over. 'This is the heir,' they said. 'Let's kill him, and the inheritance will be ours.' So they threw him out of the vineyard and killed him.

"Therefore when the owner of the vineyard comes what will he do to those tenants?"

"He will bring those wretches to a wretched end," they replied, "and he will rent the vineyard to other tenants, who will give him his share of the crop at harvest time."

Jesus said to them, "Have you never read in the Scriptures"

" 'The stone the builders rejected

has become the capstone;

the Lord had done this,

and it is marvelous in our eyes'?

"Therefore I tell you that the kingdom of God will be taken away from you and given to a people who will produce its fruit. He who falls on this stone will be broken to pieces, but he on whom it falls will be crushed."

When the chief priests and the Pharisees heard Jesus' parables, they knew he was talking about them. They looked for a way to arrest him immediately, but they were afraid of the crowd because the people held that he was a prophet. So they left him and went away.

(Mt. 22:1-14)

Jesus spoke to them again in parables, saying: "The kingdom of heaven is like a king who prepared a wedding banquet for his son. He sent his servants to those who had been invited to the banquet to tell them to come, but they refused to come.

"Then he sent some more servants and said, "Tell those who have been invited that I have prepared my dinner: My oxen and fattened cattle have been butchered, and everything is ready. Come to the wedding banquet.'

"But they paid not attention and went off-one to his field, another to his business. The rest seized his servants, mistreated them and killed them. The king was enraged. He sent his army and destroyed those murderers and burned their city.

"Then he said to his servants, 'the wedding banquet is ready, but those I invited did not deserve to come. Go to the street corners and invite to the banquet anyone you find.' So the servants went out into the streets and gathered all the people they could find, both good and bad, and the wedding hall was filled with guests.

"But when the king came in to see the guests, he noticed a man there who was not wearing wedding clothes. 'Friend', he asked, 'how did you get in here without wedding clothes?" The man was speechless.

"Then the king told the attendants, 'Tie him hand and foot, and throw him outside, into the darkness, where there will be weeping and gnashing of teeth.' For many are invited, but few are chosen."

(Mt. 22:15-22/Mk. 12:13-17/Lk. 20:20-26)

Then the Pharisees went out and laid plans to trap him in his words. Keeping a close watch on him, they sent their disciples to him along with the Herodians as spies who pretended to be honest. They hoped to catch Jesus in something he said so that they might hand him over to the power and authority of the governor.

So the spies questioned him, "Teacher, we know that you speak and teach what is right, you are a man of integrity and that you teach the way of God in accordance with the truth. You aren't swayed by men, because you pay no attention to who they are. Tell us then, what is your opinion? Is it right to pay taxes to Caesar or not?"

He saw through their duplicity and said to them, "You hypocrites, why are you trying to trap me? Bring me a denarius and let me look at it." They brought the coin, and he asked them, "Whose portrait is this? And whose inscription?"

"Caesar's." they replied.

Then Jesus said to them, "Give to Caesar what is Caesar's and to God what is God's."

They were unable to trap him in what he had said there in public. And astonished by his answer they became silent. Then they left him and went away.

(Mt. 22:23-33/Mk. 12:18-27/Lk. 20:27-39)

That day some of the Sadducees who say there is no resurrection came to him with a question. "Teacher" they said. "Moses wrote for us that if a man's brother dies and leaves a wife but no children, the man must marry the widow and have children for his brother. Now there were seven brothers among us. The first one married and died, and since he had no children, he left his wife to his brother.

The second one married the widow, but he also died, leaving no child. It was the same with the third. In fact, none of the seven left any children. Last of all, the woman died too. At the resurrection when men rise from the dead whose wife will she be, since the seven were married to her?"

Jesus replied, "Are you not in error because you do not know the Scriptures or the power of God? When the dead rise, they will neither marry nor be given in marriage; they will be like the angels in heaven. The people of this age marry and are given in marriage. But those who are considered worthy of taking part in that age and in the resurrection from the dead will neither marry nor be given in marriage, and they can no longer die; for they are like the angels. They are God's children, since they are children of the resurrection. But in the account of the bush, even Moses showed that the dead rise, for he calls the Lord 'the God of Abraham, and the God of Isaac, and the God of Jacob.' He is not the God of the dead, but of the living, for to him all are alive in the book of Moses. You are badly mistaken."

Some of the teachers of the law responded, "Well said, teacher!" When the crowds heard this, they were astonished at his teaching.

(Mt. 22:34-40/Mk. 12:28-34)

Hearing that Jesus had silenced the Sadducees, the Pharisees got together. One of the teachers of the law came and heard them debating. Noticing that Jesus had given them a good answer, he asked him, "Of all the commandments, which is the most important?"

"The most important one," answered Jesus, "is this; 'Hear, O Israel, the Lord our God, the Lord is one. Love the Lord your God with all your heart and with all your soul and with all your mind and with all your strength.' The second is this: 'Love your neighbor as yourself.' All the Law and the Prophets hang on these two commandments. There is no commandment greater than these."

"Well said, teacher," the man replied. "You are right in saying that God is one and there is no other but him. To love him with all your heart, with all your understanding and with all your strength, and to love your neighbor as yourself is more important than all burnt offerings and sacrifices."

When Jesus saw that he had answered wisely, he said to him, "You are not far from the kingdom of God."

(Mt. 22:41-46/Mk. 12:34-37/Lk. 20:40-44)

While Jesus was teaching in the temple courts, while Pharisees were gathered together, Jesus asked them, "What do you think about the Christ? Whose son is he?"

"The son of David," they replied.

He said to them, "How is it then that David, speaking by the Spirit, calls him 'Lord'? For David himself declares in the book of Psalms:

" 'The Lord said to my Lord:

"Sit at my right hand

until I put your enemies

under your feet." '

"If then David calls him 'Lord,' how can he be his son?" No one could say a word in reply, and from that day on no one dared to ask him any more questions. The large crowd listened to him with delight.

(Mt. 23:1-36/Mk. 12:38-40/Lk. 11:42-54, 20:45-47)

Then Jesus said to the crowds and to his disciples: "The teachers of the law and the Pharisees sit in Moses' seat. So you must obey them and do everything they tell you. But do not do what they do, for they do not practice what they preach. They tie up heavy loads and put them on men's shoulders, but they themselves are not willing to lift a finger to move them.

"Everything they do is done for men to see: They make their phylacteries wide and the tassels on their garments long; they like to walk around in flowing robes they love the place of honor at banquets and the most important seats in the synagogues; they love to be greeted in the marketplaces and to have men call them 'Rabbi.'

"But you are not to be called 'Rabbi,' for you have only one Master and you are all brothers. And do not call anyone on earth 'father,' for you have one Father, and he is in heaven. Nor are you to be called 'teacher,' for you have one Teacher, the Christ. The greatest among you will be your servant. For whoever exalts himself will be humbled, and whoever humbles himself will be exalted.

"Woe to you, teachers of the law and Pharisees, you hypocrites! You shut the kingdom of heaven in men' faces. You yourselves do not enter, nor will you let those enter who are trying to.

"Woe to you, teachers of the Law and Pharisees, you hypocrites! You devour widows' houses and for a show make lengthy prayers therefore you will be punished more severely.

"Woe to you, teachers of the law and Pharisees, you hypocrites! You travel over land and sea to win a single convert, and when he becomes one, you make him twice as much a son of hell as you are.

"Woe to you, blind guides! You say, 'If anyone swears by the temple, it means nothing; but if anyone swears by the gold of the temple, he is bound by his oath.' You blind fools! Which is greater; the gold, or the temple that makes the gold sacred? You also say, 'If anyone swears by the altar, it means nothing; but if anyone swears by the gift on it, he is bound by his oath.' You blind men! Which is greater; the gift, or the altar that makes the gift sacred? Therefore, he who swears by the altar swears by it and by everything on it. And he who swears by the temple swears by it and by the one who dwells in it. And he who swears by heaven swears by God's throne and by the one who sits on it.

"Woe to you, teachers of the law and Pharisees, you hypocrites! You give a tenth of your spices-mint, dill and cummin. But you have neglected the more important matters of the law – justices, mercy and faithfulness. You should have practiced the latter, without neglecting the former. You blind guides! You strain out a gnat but swallow a camel.

"Woe to you, teachers of the law and Pharisees, you hypocrites! You clean the outside of the cup and dish, but inside they are full of greed and self-indulgence. Blind Pharisee! First clean the inside of the cup and dish, and then the outside also will be clean.

"Woe to you, teachers of the law and Pharisees, you hypocrites! You are like whitewashed tombs, which look beautiful on the outside but on the inside are full of dead men's bones and everything unclean. In the same way, on the outside you appear to people as righteous but on the inside you are full of hypocrisy and wickedness.

"Woe to you, because you are like unmarked graves, which men walk over without knowing it."

One of the experts in the law answered him, "Teacher, when you say these things, you insult us also."

Jesus replied, "And you experts in the law woe to you, because you load people down with burdens they can hardly carry, and you yourselves will not lift one finger to help them.

"Woe to you, teachers of the law and Pharisees, you hypocrites! You build tombs for the prophets and decorate the graves of the righteous. And you say, 'If we had lived in the days of our forefathers, we would not have taken part with them in shedding the blood of the prophets.' So you testify against yourselves that you are the descendants of those who murdered the prophets. They killed the prophets, and you build their tombs. Fill up, then, the measure of the sin of your forefathers!

"You snakes! You brood of vipers! How will you escape being condemned to hell? Because of this, God in his wisdom said: Therefore I am sending you prophets and apostles, wise men and teachers. Some of them you will kill and crucify; others you will flog in your synagogues and pursue from town to town. And so upon you will come all the righteous blood that has been shed on earth, from the blood of Abel to the blood of Zechariah son of Berekiah, whom you murdered between the temple and the altar. I tell you the truth, all this will come upon this generation.

"Woe to you experts in the law, because you have taken away the key to knowledge. You yourselves have not entered, and you have hindered those who were entering."

When Jesus left there, the Pharisees and the teachers of the law began to oppose him fiercely and to besiege him with questions, waiting to catch him in something he might say.

(Mt. 23:37-39/Lk. 13:31-35)

At that time some Pharisees came to Jesus and said to him, "Leave this place and go somewhere else. Herod wants to kill you."

He replied, "Go tell that fox, 'I will drive out demons and heal people today and tomorrow, and on the third day I will reach my goal.' In any case, I must keep going today and tomorrow and the next – day for surely no prophet can die outside Jerusalem!

"O Jerusalem, Jerusalem, you who kill the prophets and stone those sent to you, how often I have longed to gather your children together, as a hen gathers her chicks under her wings, but you were not willing! Look, your house is left to you desolate. I tell you, you will not see me again until you say, 'Blessed is he who comes in the name of the Lord.' "

(Mk. 12:41-44/Lk. 21:1-4)

Jesus sat down opposite the place where the offerings were put and watched the crowd putting their money into the temple treasury. Many rich people threw in large amounts. But a poor widow came and put in two very small copper coins, worth only a fraction of a penny.

Calling his disciples to him, Jesus said, "I tell you the truth, this poor widow had put more in to the treasury than all the others. All these people gave their gifts out of their wealth; but she gave out of her poverty put in all she had to live on."

(Mt. 24:1-14/Mk. 13:1-13/Lk. 21:5-19)

Jesus left the temple and was walking away when one of his disciples said to him, "Look, Teacher! What massive stones! What magnificent buildings!"

"Do you see all these great buildings?" replied Jesus. "Time will come when not one stone here will be left on another; every one will be thrown down."

As Jesus was sitting on the Mount of Olives opposite the temple, Peter, James, John and Andrew asked him privately:[4]

"Tell us when will this happen? And what will be the sign that they are all about to be fulfilled, what will be the sign of your coming and of the end of the age?"

Jesus answered, "Watch out that no one deceives you. For many will come in my name, claiming, 'I am the Christ. And 'The time is near.' and will deceive many. Do not follow them.

"When you hear of wars and rumors of wars, and of revolutions, but see to it that you are not alarmed. Such things must happen, but the end is still to come. Nation will rise against nation, and kingdom against kingdom. There will be famines, great earthquakes and pestilences in various places and fearful events and great signs from heaven. All these are the beginning of birth pains.

"You must be on your guard. But before all this, they will lay hands on you and persecute you. They will deliver you to synagogues and prisons, and you will be brought before kings and governors, and all on account of my name.

"At that time many will turn away from the faith and will betray and hate each other, and many false prophets will appear and deceive many people. Because of the increase of wickedness, the love of most will grow cold.

"Brother will betray brother to death, and a father his child. Children will rebel against their parents and have them put to death and they will put some of you to death. But not a hair of your head will perish. By standing firm you will gain life. He who stands firm to the end will be saved. You will be hated by all nations because of me. This will result in your being witnesses to them. Whenever you are arrested and brought to trial, do not worry beforehand about what to say.

"For I will give you words and wisdom that none of your adversaries will be able to resist or contradict. Just say whatever is given you at the time, for it is not you speaking, but the Holy Spirit. And this gospel of the kingdom will be preached in the whole world as a testimony to all nations, and then the end will come.

(Mt. 24:15-28, 37-41/Mk. 13:14-23/Lk. 17:22-37, 21:20-25)

"When you see Jerusalem being surrounded by armies, you will know that its desolation is near.

"So, when you see standing in the holy place 'the abomination that causes desolation,' spoken of through the prophet Daniel – let the reader understand. Then let those who are in Judea flee to the mountains, let those in the city get out, and let those in the country not enter the city.

"Let no one on the roof of his house go down or enter the house to take anything out. Let no one in the field to back to get his cloak.

"For this is the time of punishment in fulfillment of all that has been written. How dreadful it will be in those days for pregnant women and nursing mothers!

"Pray that your flight will not take place in winter or on the Sabbath. Because those will be days of distress unequaled from the beginning, when God created the world, until now – and never to be equaled again.

"There will be great distress in the land and wrath against this people. They will fall by the sword and will betaken as prisoners to all the nations. Jerusalem will be trampled on by the Gentiles until the times of the Gentiles are fulfilled.

"There will be signs in the sun, moon and stars. On the earth, nations will be in anguish and perplexity at the roaring and tossing of the sea.

"If the Lord had not cut short those days, no one would survive. But for the sake of the elect, whom he has chosen, he has shortened them.

"The time is coming when you will long to see one of the days of the Son of Man, but you will not see it. At that time if anyone says to you, 'Look, here is the Christ!' or, 'There he is!' do not believe it. For false Christ and false prophets will appear and perform great signs and miracles to deceive even the elect – if that were possible. So be on your guard; I have told you everything ahead of time.

"So if anyone tells you, 'There he is, out in the desert,' do not go out; or, 'Here he is, in the inner rooms,' do not believe it.

"For the Son of Man in his day will be like the lightning, which flashes and lights up the sky from one end to the other. But first he must suffer many things and be rejected by this generation.

"Just as it was in the days of Noah, so also will it be in the days of the Son of Man. People where eating, drinking, marrying and being given in marriage up to the day Noah entered the ark. Then the flood came and destroyed them all. It was the same in the days of Lot. People were eating and drinking, buying and selling, planting and building. But the day Lot left Sodom, fire and sulfur rained down from heaven and destroyed them all.

"It will be just like this on the day of Son of Man is revealed. On that day no one who is on the roof of his house, with his goods inside, should go down to get them. Likewise, no one in the field should go back for anything. Remember Lot's wife! Whoever tries to keep his life will loose it. Whoever loses his life will preserve it. I tell you, on that night two people will be in one bed; one will be taken and the other left. Two women will be grinding grain together; one will be taken and the other left. Two men will be in the field: One will be taken and the other left."

"Where, Lord?" they asked.

He replied, "Where there is a dead body, there the vultures will gather."

(Mt. 24:29-36/Mk. 13:24-33/Lk. 21:26-36)

"But in those days, following that distress,

" 'the sun will be darkened,

and the moon will not give its light;

the stars will fall from the sky,

and the heavenly bodies will be shaken.'

"Men will faint from terror, apprehensive of what is coming on the world. At that time the sign of the Son of Man will appear in the sky, and all the nations of the earth will mourn. They will see the Son of Man coming on the clouds of the sky, with power and great glory. And he will send his angels with a loud trumpet call and gather his elect from the four winds, from the ends of the earth to the ends of the heavens.

"When these things begin to take place, stand up and lift up your heads, because your redemption is drawing near."

He told them this parable; "Look at the fig tree and all the trees. When they sprout leaves, you can see for yourselves and know that summer is near.

"Even so, when you see these things happening, you know that it is near, right at the door. I tell you the truth, this generation, will certainly not pass away until all these things have happened. Heaven and earth will pass away, but my words will never pass away.

"No one knows about that day or hour, not even the angels in heaven, nor the Son, but only the Father. Be on guard! Be alert! You do not know when that time will come.

"Be careful, or your hearts will be weighed down with dissipation, drunkenness and the anxieties of life, and that day will close on you unexpectedly like a trap. For it will come upon all those who live on the face of the whole earth. Be always on the watch, and pray that you may be able to escape all that is about to happen, and that you may be able to stand before the Son of Man."

(Mt. 24:42-26:5/Mk. 13:34-14:2/Lk. 12:35-48, 19:11-27, 22:1,2)

"Therefore keep watch, because you do not know on what day your lord will come. Be dressed ready for service and keep your lamps burning, like men waiting for their master to return from a wedding banquet, so that when he comes and knocks they can immediately open the door for him. It will be good for those servants whose master finds them watching when he comes. I tell you the truth, he will dress himself to serve, will have them recline at the table and will come and wait on them. It will be good for those servants whose master finds them ready, even if he comes in the second or third watch of the night. But understand this: If the owner of the house had known at what hour the thief was coming, he would not have let his house be broken into. You also must be ready, because the Son of Man will come at an hour when you do not expect him."

Peter asked, "Lord, are you telling this parable to us, or to everyone?"

The Lord answered, "Who then is the faithful and wise manager, whom the master puts in charge of his servants to give them their food allowance at the proper time? It will be good for that servant whom the master finds doing so when he returns. I tell you the truth, he will put him in charge of all his possessions. But suppose the servant says to himself, 'My master is taking a long time in coming,' and he then begins to beat the menservants and maidservants and to eat and drink and eat drunk. The master of that servant will come on a day when he does not expect him and at an hour he is not aware of. He will cut him to pieces and assign him a place with the unbelievers.

"That servant who knows his master's will and does not get ready or does not do what his master wants will be beaten with many blows. But the one who does not know and does things deserving punishment will be beaten with few blows. From everyone who has been given much, much will be demanded; and from the one who has been entrusted with much, much more will be asked.

"Therefore keep watch because you do not know when the owner of the house will come back – whether in the evening, or at midnight, or when the rooster crows, or at dawn. If he comes suddenly, do not let him find you sleeping. What I say to you, I say to everyone: 'Watch!' "

"At that time the kingdom of heaven will be like ten virgins who took their lamps and went out to meet the bridegroom. Five of them were foolish and five were wise. The foolish ones took their lamps but did not take any oil with them. The wise, however, took oil in jars along with their lamps. The bridegroom was a long time in coming, and they all became drowsy and fell asleep.

"At midnight the cry rang out: 'here's the bridegroom! Come out to meet him!'

"Then all the virgins woke up and trimmed their lamps. The foolish ones said to the wise, 'Give us some of you roil; our lamps are going out.'

" 'No,' they replied, 'there may not be enough for both us and you. Instead, go to those who sell oil and buy some for yourselves.'

"But while they were on their way to buy the oil, the bridegroom arrived. The virgins who were ready went in with him to the wedding banquet. And the door was shut.

"Later the others also came. 'Sir! Sir!' they said. 'Open the door for us!'

"But he replied, 'I tell you the truth, I don't know you.'"

While they were listening to this, he went on to tell them a parable, because he was near Jerusalem and the people thought that the kingdom of God was going to appear at once.

"Therefore keep watch, because you do not know the day or the hour."

He said: "Again it will be like a man of noble birth went to a distant country to have himself appointed king and then to return. So he called his servants and entrusted his property to them. To one he gave five talents of money,[5] to another two talents, and to another one talent, each according to his ability. 'Put this money to work,' he said, 'until I come back.' Then he went on his journey.

"But his subjects hated him and sent a delegation after him to say, 'We don't want this man to be our king.'

The man who had received the five talents went at once and put his money to work and gained five more. So also, the one with the two talents gained two more. But the man who had received the one talent went off, dug a hole in the ground and hid his master's money.

"After a long time the master of those servants who was made king returned home.

"Then he sent for the servants to whom he had given the money, in order to find out what they had gained with it. The man who had received the five talents brought the other five. 'Master,' he said, 'you entrusted me with five talents. See, I have gained five more.' 'Well done my good and faithful servant!' his master replied. 'Because you have been trustworthy in a very small matter, take charge of ten cities. Come and share your master's happiness!'

"The man with two talents also came. 'Master,' he said, 'you entrusted me with two talents; see, I have gained two more.'

"His master replied, 'Well done, good and faithful servant! You have been faithful with a few things; I will put you in charge of many things. You take charge of five cities. Come and share your master's happiness!'

"Then the man who had received the one talent came. 'Master,' he said, 'I knew that you are a hard man, harvesting where you have not sown and gathering where you have not scattered seed. So I was afraid and went out and hid your talent in the ground. See, here is what belongs to you.'

"His master replied, 'I will judge you by your own words, you wicked, lazy servant! So you knew that I harvest where I have not sown and gather where I have not scattered seed? Well then, you should have put my money on deposit with the bankers, so that when I returned I would have received it back with interest.'

"Then he said to those standing by 'Take the talent from him and give it to the one who has the ten talents.' 'Sir,' they said, 'he already has ten!' He replied, 'I tell you that to everyone who has will be given more, and he will have an abundance. Whoever does not have, even what he had will be taken from him. And throw that worthless servant outside, into the darkness, where there will be weeping and gnashing of teeth.'

"But those enemies of mine who did not want me to be king over them – bring them here and kill them in front of me.' "

"When the Son of Man comes in his glory, and all the angels with him, he will sit on his throne in heavenly glory. All the nations will be gathered before him, and he will separate the people one from another as a shepherd separates the sheep from the goats. He will put the sheep on his right and the goats on his left.

"Then the King will say to those on his right, 'come, you who are blessed by my Father; take your inheritance, the kingdom prepared for you since the creation of the world. For I was hungry and you gave me something to eat, I was thirsty and you gave me something to drink, I was a stranger and you invited me in, I needed clothes and you clothed me, I was sick and you looked after me, I was in prison and you came to visit me.'

"Then the righteous will answer him, 'Lord, when did we see you hungry and feed you, or thirsty and give you something to drink? When did we see you a stranger and invite you in, or needing clothes and clothe you? When did we see you sick or in prison and go to visit you?'

"The King will reply, 'I tell you the truth, whatever you did for one of the least or these brothers of mine, you did for me.'

"Then he will say to those on his left, 'Depart from me, you who are cursed, into the eternal fire prepared for the devil and his angels. For I was hungry and you gave me nothing to eat, I was thirsty and you gave me nothing to drink, I was a stranger and you did not invite me in, I needed clothes and you did not clothe me, I was sick and in prison and you did not look after me.'

"They also will answer, 'Lord, when did we see you hungry or thirsty or a stranger or needing clothes or sick or in prison, and did not help you?'

"He will reply, 'I tell you the truth, whatever you did not do for one of the least of these, you did not do for me.'

"Then they will go away to eternal punishment, but the righteous to eternal life."

When Jesus had finished saying all these things, he said to his disciples, "As you know, the Passover is two days away – and they Son of Man will be handed over to be crucified."[6]

[*As Jesus was talking with his disciples in the Mount of Olives, that very same night in Jerusalem....*]

Then the chief priests and the elders of the people assembled in the palace of the high priest, whose name was Caiaphas, and they plotted to arrest Jesus in some sly way and kill him. "But not during the Feast," they said, "or there may be a riot among the people."[7]

(Lk 19:47,48, 21:37,38)

[8]Every day he was teaching at the temple. Each day Jesus was teaching at the temple, and each evening he went out to spend the night on the hill called the Mount of Olives, and all the people came early in the morning to hear him at the temple.

But the chief priests, the teachers of the law and the leaders among the people were trying to kill him. Yet they could not find any way to do it, because all the people hung on his words.

(Jn. 12: 20-50)

[*The following could have happened on any day between Sunday to Thursday of the holy week*]

Now there were some Greeks among those who went up to worship at the Feast. They came to Philip, who was from Bethsaida in Galilee, with a request. "Sir," they said, "we would like to see Jesus." Philip went to tell Andrew; Andrew and Philip in turn told Jesus.

Jesus replied, "The hour has come for the Son of Man to be glorified. I tell you the truth, unless a kernel of wheat falls to the ground and dies, it remains only a single seed. But if it dies, it produces many seeds. The man who loves his life will lose it, while the man who hates his life in this world will keep it for eternal life. Whoever serves me must follow me; and where I am, my servant also will be. My Father will honor the one who serves me.

"Now my heart is troubled, and what shall I say? 'Father, save me from this hour'? No, it was for this very reason I came to this hour. Father, glorify your name!"

Then a voice came from heaven, "I have glorified it, and will glorify it again."[9] The crowd that was there and heard it said it had thundered; others said an angel had spoken to him.

Jesus said, "This voice was for your benefit, not mine. Now is the time for judgment on this world; now the prince of this world will be driven out. But I, when I am lifted up from the earth, will draw all men to myself."[10] He said this to show the kind of death he was going to die.

The crowd spoke up, "We have heard from the Law that the Christ will remain forever, so how can you say, 'The Son of Man must be lifted up'? Who is this 'Son of Man'?"

The Jesus told them, "You are going to have the light just a little while longer. Walk while you have the light, before darkness overtakes you. The man who walks in the dark does not know where he is going. Put your trust in the light while you have it, so that you may become sons of light." When he had finished speaking, Jesus left and hid himself from them.

Even after Jesus had done all these miraculous signs in their presence, they still would not believe in him. This was to fulfill the word of Isaiah the prophet:

"Lord, who has believed our message
and to whom has the arm of the Lord been
revealed?"

For this reason they could not believe, because, as Isaiah says elsewhere:

"He has blinded their eyes
and deadened their hears,
so they can neither see with their eyes,
nor understand with their hearts,
nor turn-and I would heal them."

Isaiah said this because he saw Jesus' glory and spoke about him.

Yet at the same time many even among the leaders believed in him. But because of the Pharisees they would not confess their faith for fear they would be put out of the synagogue; for they loved praise from men more than praise from God.

Then Jesus cried out, "When a man believes in me, he does not believe in me only, but in the one who sent me. When he looks at me, he sees the one who sent me. I have come into the world as a light, so that no one who believes in me should stay in darkness.

"As for the person who hears my words but does not keep them, I do not judge him. For I did not come to judge the world, but to save it. There is a judge for the one who rejects me and does not accept my words; that very word which I spoke will condemn him at the last day. For I did not speak of my own accord, but the Father who sent me commanded me what to say and how to say it. I know that his command leads to eternal life. So whatever I say is just what the Father has told me to say."

STUDY NOTES

1. Only on the next day morning the disciples notice that the fig tree had withered. Either they failed to notice the withered fig tree on their return the same day evening or the fig tree withered only after last evening.

2. This instruction is for a situation when one holds anything against others.

See Chapter 9 Study Note No: 4 for the opposite situation.

3. This is the fourth and final time that Jesus bears witness for John the Baptist. The other incidents are:

First time Chapter 7 Study Note No: 3

Second time Chapter 13 Study Note No: 2

Third time Chapter 18 Study Note No: 7

4. John the only eyewitness to this event, wrote one of the four gospels. Yet this event does not find any mention at all in John's gospel! For similar occurrence see:

Chapter 18 Study Note No: 3

Chapter 21 Study Note No: 2

5. Matthew in his account explains in detail that the master gave 5, 2 and 1 talents to three of his servants respectively. But Luke in his gospel just mentions that the master gave ten minas to ten servants. Therefore the more detailed description of the two has been taken into account.

6. This is the sixth time Jesus is fore telling His suffering and death.

7. The plan to kill Jesus is put on hold temporarily. For the reversal of this decision see Chapter 26 Study Note No: 3

8. This was His daily routine from Sunday to Thursday of that week.

9. This is the third and final time there is a voice from the heaven during the earthly ministry of Jesus. For the earlier two occasions see:

Chapter 4 Study Note No: 3

Chapter 18 Study Note No: 2

10. Jesus has said this before. See Chapter 5 Study Note No: 2

XXVI
MARY PAYS HER (LAST) RESPECT (WEDNESDAY)

(Mt. 26:6-16/Mk. 14:3-11/Lk. 22:3-6/Jn. 12:2-8)

[1] While Jesus was in Bethany in the home of a man known as Simon the Leper. A dinner was given in Jesus' honor. Martha served, while Lazarus was among those reclining at the table with him. Then Mary came with an alabaster jar or about a pint of pure nard, an expensive perfume. She broke the jar poured the perfume on Jesus' head and feet and wiped his feet[2] with her hair. And the house was filled with the fragrance of the perfume.

But one of his disciples, Judas Iscariot, who was later to betray him, objected, "Why wasn't this perfume sold and the money given to the poor? It was worth a year's wages." He did not say this because he cared about the poor but because he was a thief; as keeper of the money bag, he used to help himself to what was put into it.

"Leave her alone," Jesus replied. "Why are you bothering this woman? She has done a beautiful thing to me. It was intended that she should save this perfume for the day of my burial.

"The poor you will always have with you, and you can help them any time you want. But you will not always have me. She did what she could. She poured perfume on my body beforehand to prepare for my burial. I tell you the truth, wherever the gospel is preached throughout the world, what she had done will also be told, in memory of her."

Then Satan entered Judas, called Iscariot, one of the Twelve. And Judas went to the chief priests and the officers of the temple guard and discussed with them how he might betray Jesus. They were delighted and agreed to give him money.[3] He consented, and watched for an opportunity to hand Jesus over to them when no crowd was present.

(Jn. 13:1)

It was just before the Passover Feast. Jesus knew that the time had come for him to leave this world and go to the Father. Having loved his own who were in the world, he loved them to the last.

STUDY NOTES

1. When the following points are considered, one gets an impression that two identical incidents have taken place:

a. When Jesus came to Bethany (Saturday) a dinner was given in His honor. Mary poured an expensive perfume on Jesus feet and wiped His feet with hair. (Jn 12:1-8)

b. A woman poured very expensive perfume on Jesus head when He was at the house of Simon, the leper in Bethany. This was on Wednesday i.e., a day after the religious leaders had put on hold the plan to kill Jesus. (Mt 26:3-7/ Mk 14:1-3)

When we read the above said portions it appears that there had been two dinners hosted in Jesus' honor i.e., on the nights of Saturday and Wednesday. And it also seems that Mary was one of the women anointing the feet of Jesus while the other women His head.

This confusion is resolved as follows:

On closer observation of the related passages it is clear that none of the four gospels state that Jesus was anointed twice on the last week. Moreover the comments of the disciples to this event and the response of Jesus to their comments are too similar to confirm this as two different incidents. Judas volunteers to betray Jesus only after this response of Jesus. And the religious leaders revive their plan to kill Jesus only after his offer. Therefore this incident of anointing has to have happened on Wednesday i.e., after Tuesday when the plot to kill was put on hold.

Since Jn 12:1, 2 simply states that dinner was hosted in Jesus' honor in Bethany without specifically stating that it was hosted on the same day of His arrival i.e., Saturday, there is no reason to believe so. Therefore it is concluded that there was only one dinner hosted in Jesus honor in the last week and that was on Wednesday in the house of Simon, the leper at Bethany. Mary not only anointed Jesus' feet but also His head. This conclusion does not contradict any of the details given in the three gospel accounts Mt. 26:8-13/Mk. 14:4-9/Jn. 12:4-8 respectively.

2. Mary is the second woman to thus honor Jesus. The first one to do so is seen in Chapter 13 Study Note No: 3

3. The murder plan that was put on hold the previous day is revived upon Judas' offer. See Chapter 25 Study Note No: 7

XXVII
THE LAST PASSOVER OF JESUS CHRIST (THURSDAY)

Day: 6 THURSDAY:

(Mt. 26:17-35/Mk. 14:12-31/Lk. 22:7-39/Jn. 13:2-17:26)

Then came the day of Unleavened Bread on which the Passover lamb had to be sacrificed. Jesus sent Peter and John, saying, "Go and make preparations for us to eat the Passover."

"Where do you want us to prepare for it?" they asked.

He replied, "As you enter the city, a man carrying a jar of water will meet you. Follow him to the house that he enters, and say to the owner of the house, 'The Teacher says: My appointed time is near. I am going to celebrate the Passover with my disciples at your house. Where is the guest room, where I may eat the Passover with my disciples?' He will show you a large upper room, all furnished and ready. Make preparations for us there."

The disciples left, went into the city and found things just as Jesus had told them. So they prepared the Passover.

When evening came, Jesus arrived with the Twelve.

The evening meal was being served, and the devil had already prompted Judas Iscariot, son of Simon, to betray Jesus. Jesus knew that the Father had put all things under his power, and that he had come from God and was returning to God; so he got up from the meal, took off his outer clothing, and wrapped a towel around his waist. After that, he poured water into a basin and began to wash his disciples' feet, drying them with the towel that was wrapped around him.

He came to Simon Peter, who said to him, "Lord, are you going to wash my feet?"

Jesus replied, "You do not realize now what I am doing, but later you will understand."

"No," said Peter, "you shall never wash my feet."

Jesus answered, "Unless I wash you, you have no part with me."

"Then, Lord," Simon Peter replied, "not just my feet but my hands and my head as well!"

Jesus answered, "A person who has had a bath needs only to wash his feet; his whole body is clean. And you are clean, though not every one of you." For he knew who was going to betray him, and that was why he said not everyone was clean.

When he had finished washing their feet, he put on his clothes and returned to his place. "Do you understand what I have done for you?" he asked them. "You call me 'Teacher' and 'Lord,' and rightly so, for that is what I am. Now that I, your Lord and Teacher, have washed your feet, you also should wash one another's feet. I have set you an example that you should do as I have done for you. I tell you the truth, no servant is greater than his master, nor is a messenger greater than the one who sent him. Now that you know these things, you will be blessed if you do them.

"I am not referring to all of you; I know those I have chosen. But this is to fulfill the scripture: 'He who shares my bread has lifted up his heel against me.'

"I am telling you now before it happens, so that when it does happen you will believe that I am He. I tell you the truth, whoever accepts anyone I send accepts me; and whoever accepts me accepts the one who sent me."

After he had said this, Jesus was troubled in spirit and testified, "I tell you the truth, one of you is going to betray me."

His disciples stared at one another, at a loss to know which of them he meant. They were very sad and began to say to him one after the other, "Surely not I, Lord?"

Jesus replied, "The one who has dipped his hand into the bowl with me will betray me. The Son of Man will go just as it is written about him. But woe to that man who betrays the Son of Man! It would be better for him if he had not been born."

Then Judas, the one who would betray him, said, "Surely not I, Rabbi?" (Jesus answered, "You yourself have said it.")

One of them, the disciple whom Jesus loved, was reclining next to him. Simon Peter motioned to this disciple and said, "Ask him which one he means."

Leaning back against Jesus, he asked him, "Lord, who is it?"

Jesus answered, "It is the one to whom I will give this piece of bread when I have dipped it in the dish." Then, dipping the piece of bread, he gave it to Judas Iscariot, son of Simon. As soon as Judas took the bread, Satan entered into him.

"What you are about to do, do quickly," Jesus told him, but no one at the meal understood why Jesus said this to him. Since Judas had charge of the money, some thought Jesus was telling him to buy what was needed for the Feast, or to give something to the poor. As soon as Judas had taken the bread, he went out. And it was night.

While they were eating, he said to them, "I have eagerly desired to eat this Passover with you before I suffer. For I tell you, I will not eat it again until it finds fulfillment in the kingdom of God." After taking the cup, he gave thanks and said, "Take this and divide it among you. Jesus took bread, gave thanks and broke it, and gave it to them, saying, "This is my body given for you; do this in remembrance of me."

In the same way after the supper he took the cup, gave thanks and offered it to them, saying, "Drink from it, all of you. This is my blood of the new covenant, which is poured out for many for the forgiveness of sins. I tell you, I will not drink of this fruit of the vine from now on until that day when I drink it a new with you in my Father's kingdom."

"Now is the Son of Man glorified and God is glorified in him. If God is glorified in him, God will glorify the Son in himself, and will glorify him at once.

"My children, I will be with you only a little longer. You will look for me, and just as I told the Jews, so I tell you now: Where I am going, you cannot come.

"A new command I give you: Love one another. As I have loved you, so you must love one another. By this all men will know that you are my disciples, if you love one another."

Simon Peter asked him, "Lord, where are you going?"

Jesus replied, "Where I am going, you cannot follow now, but you will follow later."

Peter asked, "Lord, why can't I follow you now? I will lay down my life for you."

"Do not let your hearts be troubled. Trust in God; trust also in me. In my Father's house are many rooms; if it were not so, I would have told you. I am going there to prepare a place for you. And if I go and prepare a place for you, I will come back and take you to be with me that you also maybe where I am. You know the way to the place where I am going."

Thomas said to him, "Lord, we don't know where you are going, so how can we know the way?"

Jesus answered, "I am the way and the truth and the life. No one comes to the Father except through me. If you really knew me, you would know my Father as well. From now on, you do know him and have seen him."

Philip said, "Lord, show us the Father and that will be enough for us."

Jesus answered: "Don't you know me, Philip, even after I have been among you such a long time? Anyone who has seen me has seen the Father. How can you say, 'Show us the Father'? Don't you believe that I am in the Father, and that the Father is in me? The words I say to you are not just my own. Rather, it is the Father, living in me, who is doing his work. Believe me when I say that I am in the Father and the Father is in me; or at least believe on the evidence of the miracles themselves. I tell you the truth; anyone who has faith in me will do what I have been doing. He will do even greater things than these, because I am going to the Father. And I will do whatever you ask in my name, so that the son may bring glory to the Father. You may ask me for anything in my name, and I will do it.

"If you love me, you will obey what I command. And I will ask the Father, and he will give you another Counselor to be with you forever – the Spirit of truth. The world cannot accept him, because it neither sees him nor knows him. But you know him, for he lives with you and will be in you. I will not leave you as orphans; I will come to you. Before long, the world will not see me anymore, but you will see me. Because I live, you also will live. On that day you will realize that I am in my Father, and you are in me, and I am in you. Whoever has my commands and obeys them, he is the one who loves me. He who loves me will be loved by my Father, and I too will love him and show myself to him."

Then Judas (not Judas Iscariot) said, "But, Lord, why do you intend to show yourself to us and not to the world?"

Jesus replied, "If anyone loves me, he will obey my teaching. My Father will love him, and we will come to him and make our home with him. He who does not love me will not obey my teaching. These words you hear are not my own; they belong to the Father who sent me.

"All this I have spoken while still with you. But the Counselor, the Holy Spirit, whom the Father will send in my name, will teach you all things and will remind you of everything I have said to you. Peace I leave with you; my peace I give you. I do not give to you as the world gives. Do not let your hearts be troubled and do not be afraid.

"You heard me say, 'I am going away and I am coming back to you.' If you loved me, you would be glad that I am going to the Father, for the Father is greater than I. I have told you now before it happens, so that when it does happen you will believe. I will not speak with you much longer, for the prince of this world is coming. He has no hold on me, but the world must learn that I love the Father and that I do exactly what my Father has commanded me. Come now; let us leave.

"When they had sung a hymn, they went out as usual to the Mount of Olives.

Then Jesus told them, "This very night you will all fall away on account of me for it is written:

" 'I will strike the shepherd,

And the sheep will be scattered.'

But after I have risen, I will go ahead of you into Galilee."

"Simon, Simon, Satan has asked to sift you as wheat. But I have prayed for you, Simon, that your faith may not fail. And when you have turned back, strengthen your brothers."

But he replied Lord, "Even if all fall away on account of you, I never will. I am ready to go with you to prison and to death."

Then Jesus answered, "Will you really lay down your life for me?[1] I tell you the truth, before the rooster crows, you will disown me three times!"

But Peter insisted emphatically, "Even if I have to die with you, I will never disown you." And all the others said the same.

Then Jesus asked them, "When I sent you without purse, bag or sandals, did you lack anything?"

"Nothing," they answered.

He said to them, "But now if you have a purse, take it, and also a bag; and if you don't have a sword, sell your cloak and buy one. It is written: 'and he was numbered with the transgressors'; and I tell you that this must be fulfilled in me. Yes, what is written about me is reaching its fulfillment."

The disciples said, "See, Lord, here are two swords."

"That is enough," he replied.

Also a dispute arose among them as to which of them was considered to be greatest. Jesus said to them, "The kings of the Gentiles lord it over them; and those who exercise authority over them call themselves

Benefactors. But you are not to be like that. Instead, the greatest among you should be like the youngest, and the one who rules like the one who serves. For who is greater, the one who is at the table or the one who serves? Is it not the one who is at the table? But I am among you as one who serves. You are those who have stood by me in my trials. And I confer on you a kingdom, just as my Father conferred one on me, so that you may eat and drink at my table in my kingdom and sit on thrones, judging the twelve tribes of Israel.[2]

"I am the true vine, and my Father is the gardener. He cuts off every branch in me that bears no fruit, while every branch that does bear fruit he prunes so that it will be even more fruitful. You are already clean because of the word I have spoken to you. Remain in me, and I will remain in you. No branch can bear fruit by itself; it must remain in the vine. Neither can you bear fruit unless you remain in me.

"I am the vine; you are the branches. If a man remains in me and I in him, he will bear much fruit; apart from me you can do nothing. If anyone does not remain in me, he is like a branch that is thrown away and withers; such branches are picked up, thrown into the fire and burned. If you remain in me and my words remain in you, ask whatever you wish, and it will be given you. This is to my Father's glory, that you bear much fruit, showing yourselves to be my disciples.

"As the Father has loved me, so have I loved you. Now remain in my love. If you obey my commands, you will remain in my love, just as I have obeyed my Father's commands and remain in his love. I have told you this so that my joy may be in you and that your joy may be complete. My command is this: Love each other as I have loved you. Greater love has no one than this, that he lay down his life for his friends. You are my friends if you do what I command. I no longer call you servants, because a servant does not know his master's business. Instead, I have called you friends, for everything that I learned from my Father I have made known to you. You did not choose me, but I chose you and appointed you to go and bear fruit– fruit that will last. Then the Father will give you what ever you ask in my name. This is my command: Love each other.

"If the world hates you, keep in mind that it hated me first. If you belonged to the world, it would love you as its own. As it is, you do not belong to the world, but I have chosen you out of the world. That is why the world hates you. Remember the words I spoke to you: 'No servant is greater than his master.' If they persecuted me, they will persecute you also. If they obeyed my teaching, they will obey yours also. They will treat you this way because of my name, for they do not know the One who sent me. If I had not come and spoken to them, they would not be guilty of sin. Now, however, they have no excuse for their sin. He who hates me hates my Father as well. If I had not done among them what no one else did, they would not be guilty of sin. But now they have seen these miracles, and yet they have hated both me and my Father. But this is to fulfill what is written in their Law: 'They hated me without reason.'

"When the Counselor comes, whom I will send to you from the Father, the Spirit of truth who goes out from the Father, he will testify about me. And you also must testify, for you have been with me from the beginning.

"All this I have told you so that you will not go astray. They will put you out of the synagogue; in fact, a time is coming when anyone who kills you will think he is offering a service to God. They will do such things because they have not known the Father or me. I have told you this, so that when the time comes you will remember that I warned you. I did not tell you this at first because I was with you.

"Now I am going to him who sent me, yet none of you asks me, 'where are you going?' Because I have said these things, you are filled with grief. But I tell you the truth: It is for your good that I am going away. Unless I go away, the Counselor will not come to you; but if I go, I will send him to you. When he comes, he will convict the world of guilt in regard to sin and righteousness and judgment: in regard to sin, because men do not believe in me; in regard to righteousness, because I am going to the Father, where you can see me no longer; and in regard to judgment, because the prince of this world now stands condemned.

"I have much more to say to you, more than you can now bear. But when he, the Spirit of truth, comes, he will guide you into all truth. He will not speak on his own; he will speak only what he hears, and he will tell you what is yet to come. He will bring glory to me by taking from what is mine and making it known to you. All that belongs to the Father is mine. That is why I said the Spirit will take from what is mine and make it known to you.

"In a little while you will see me no more, and then after a little while you will see me."

Some of his disciples said to one another, "What does he mean by saying, 'In a little while you will see me no more, and then after a little while you will see me,' and 'Because I am going to the Father'?" They kept asking, "What does he mean by 'a little while'? We don't understand what he is saying."

Jesus saw that they wanted to ask him about this, so he said to them, "Are you asking one another what I meant when I said, 'In a little while you will see me no more, and then after a little while you will see me'? I tell you the truth, you will weep and mourn while the world rejoices. You will grieve, but your grief will turn to joy. A woman giving birth to a child has pain because her time has come; but when her baby is born she forgets the anguish because of her joy that a child is born into the world. So with you: Now is your time of grief, but I will see you again and you will rejoice, and no one will take away your joy. In that day you will no longer ask me anything. I tell you the truth, my Father will give you whatever you ask in my name. Until now you have not asked for anything in my name. Ask and you will receive, and your joy will be complete.

"Though I have been speaking figuratively, a time is coming when I will no longer use this kind of language but will tell you plainly about my Father. In that day you will ask in my name. I am not saying that I will ask the Father on your behalf. No, the Father himself loves you because you have loved me and have believed that I came from God. I came from the Father and entered the world; now I am leaving the world and going back to the Father."

Then Jesus' disciples said, "Now you are speaking clearly and without figures of speech. Now we can see that you know all things and that you do not even need to have anyone ask you questions. This makes us believe that you came from God."

"You believe at last!" Jesus answered. "But a time is coming, and has come, when you will be scattered, each to his own home. You will leave me all alone. Yet I am not alone, for my Father is with me.

"I have told you these things, so that in me you may have peace. In this world you will have trouble. But take heart! I have overcome the world."

After Jesus said this, he looked toward heaven and prayed:

"Father, the time has come. Glorify your son, that your Son may glorify you. For you granted him authority over all people that he might give eternal life to all those you have given him. Now this is eternal life: that they may know you, the only true God, and Jesus Christ, whom you have sent. I have brought you glory on earth by completing the work you gave me to do. And now, Father, glorify me in your presence with the glory I had with you before the world began.

"I have revealed you to those whom you gave me out of the world. They were yours; you gave them to me and they have obeyed your word. Now they know that everything you have given me comes from you. For I gave them the words you gave me and they accepted them. They knew with certainty that I came from you, and they believed that you sent me. I pray for them. I am not praying for the world, but for those you have given me, for they are yours. All I have is yours, and all you have is mine. And glory has come to me through them. I will remain in the world no longer, but they are still in the world, and I am coming to you. Holy Father, protect them by the power of your name – the name you gave me – so that they may be one as we are one. While I was with them, I protected them and kept them safe by that name you gave me. None has been lost except the one doomed to destruction so that Scripture would be fulfilled.

"I am coming to you now, but I say these things while I am still in the world, so that they may have the full measure of my joy within them. I have given them your word and the world has hated them, for they are not of the world any more than I am of the world. My prayer is not that you take them out of the world but that you protect them from the evil one. They are not of the world, even as I am not of it. Sanctify them by the truth; your word is truth. As you sent me into the world, I have sent them into the world. For them I sanctify myself, that they too may be truly sanctified.

"My prayer is not for them alone. I pray also for those who will believe in me through their message, that all of them may me one, Father, just as you are in me and I am in you. May they also be in us so that the world may believe that you have sent me. I have given them the glory that you gave me, that they may be one as we are one: I in them and you in me. May they be brought to complete unity to let the world know that you sent me and have loved them even as you have loved me.

"Father, I want those you have given me to be with me where I am, and to see my glory, the glory you have given me because you loved me before the creation of the world.

"Righteous Father, though the world does not know you, I know you, and they know that you have sent me. I have made you known to them, and will continue to make you known in order that the love you have for me may be in them and that I myself may be in them."

STUDY NOTES

1. When Peter made such a comment for the first time Jesus did not respond. But when he said it the second time, He does respond.
2. When Jesus was saying this there were only eleven of them around Him as Judas had left them earlier.

XXVIII

THE BETRAYAL AND ARREST AT THE GARDEN OF GETHSEMANE (THURSDAY NIGHT)

Day: 6 THURSDAY:

(Mt. 26:36-56/Mk. 14:32-52/Lk. 22:40-53/Jn. 18:1-11)

When he had finished praying, Jesus left with his disciples and crossed the Kidron Valley. On the other side there was an olive grove called Gethsemane, and he and his disciples went into it.

Now Judas, who betrayed him, knew the place, because Jesus had often met there with his disciples.

Jesus said to his disciples, "Sit here while I pray." He took Peter, James and John the two sons of Zebedee along with him, and he began to be deeply distressed and troubled. "My soul is overwhelmed with sorrow to the point of death," he said to them. "Stay here and keep watch. Pray that you will not fall into temptation."

"He withdrew about a stone's throw beyond them, knelt down fell with his face down and prayed that if possible the hour might pass from him. "Abba, Father," he said, "everything is possible for you. If you are willing. Take this cup from me. Yet not what I will, but what you will."

An angel from heaven appeared to him and strengthened him. And being in anguish, he prayed more earnestly, and his sweat was like drops of blood falling to the ground.

When he rose from prayer and went back to the disciples, he found them asleep, exhausted from sorrow.

"Simon," he said to Peter, "are you asleep? Could you not keep watch for one hour? Watch and pray so that you will not fall into temptation. The spirit is willing, but the body is weak."

He went away a second time and prayed, "My Father, if it is not possible for this cup to be taken away unless I drink it, may your will be done."

When he came back, he again found them sleeping, because their eyes were heavy. They did not know what to say to him. So he left them and went away once more and prayed the third time, saying the same things.

Returning the third time, he said to them, "Are you still sleeping and resting? Enough! The hour has come. Look. The Son of Man is betrayed into the hands of sinners. Rise! Let us go! Here comes my betrayer!"

While he was still speaking, Judas, one of the Twelve, came to the grove, guiding a detachment of soldiers and some officials from the chief priests and Pharisees. They were carrying torches, lanterns and weapons.

Now the betrayer had arranged a signal with them: "The one I kiss is the man; arrest him and lead him away under guard."

Jesus, knowing all that was going to happen to him, went out and asked them, "Who is it you want?"

"Jesus of Nazareth," they replied.

"I am he," Jesus said. (And Judas the traitor was standing there with them.) When Jesus said, "I am he," they drew back and fell to the ground.

Again he asked them, "Who is it you want?"

And they said, "Jesus of Nazareth."

"I told you that I am he," Jesus answered. "If you are looking for me, then let these men go." This happened so that the words he had spoken would be fulfilled: "I have not lost one of those you gave me."

Judas approached Jesus to kiss him, but Jesus asked him, "Judas, are you betraying the Son of Man with a kiss?"

Going at once to Jesus, Judas said, "Greetings, Rabbi!" and kissed him.

Jesus replied, "Friend, why have you come?"

The men seized Jesus and arrested him.

When Jesus' followers saw what was going to happen, they said, "Lord, should we strike with our swords?"

Then Simon Peter, who had a sword, drew it and struck the high priest's servant, cutting off his right ear.(The servant's name was Malchus)

But Jesus answered, "No more of this!" And he touched the man's ear and healed him."

"Put your sword back in its place," Jesus said to him, "for all who draw the sword will die by the sword. Do you think I cannot call on my Father, and he will at once put at my disposal more than twelve legions of angles? But how then would the Scriptures be fulfilled that say it must happen in this way?

"Shall I not drink the cup the Father has given me?"

Then Jesus said to the chief priests, the officers of the temple guard, and the elders, who had come for him, "Am I leading a rebellion, that you have come with swords and clubs? Every day I sat in the temple courts teaching, and you did not arrest me. But this is your hour – when darkness reigns.

"But this has all taken place that the writings of the prophets might me fulfilled." Then all the disciples deserted him and fled.

A young man, wearing nothing but a linen garment, was following Jesus. When they seized him, he fled naked, leaving his garment behind.

XXIX
THE JEWISH (TRIAL!) PLOT TO KILL (FRIDAY)

THURSDAY NIGHT:

(Mt. 26:57-75/Mk. 14:53-72/Lk. 22:54-71/Jn. 18:12-27)

Then the detachment of soldiers with its commander and the Jewish officials arrested Jesus. They bound him and brought him first to Annas,[1] who was the father-in-law of Caiaphas, the high priest that year. Caiaphas was the one who had advised the Jews that it would be good if one man died for the people.

Simon Peter and another disciple were following Jesus. Because this disciple was known to the high priest, he went with Jesus into the high priest's courtyard, but Peter had to wait outside at the door. The other disciple, who was known the high priest, came back, spoke to the girl on duty there and brought Peter in.

It was cold, and the servants and officials kindled a fire in the middle of the courtyard and had sat down together, Peter sat down with them.

Meanwhile, the high priest questioned Jesus, about his disciples and his teaching.

"I have spoken openly to the world," Jesus replied. "I always taught in synagogues or at the temple, where all the Jews come together. I said nothing to secret. Why question me? Ask those who heard me. Surely they know what I said."

When Jesus said this, one of the officials nearby struck him in the face. "Is this the way you answer the high priest?" he demanded.

"If I said something wrong," Jesus replied, "testify as to what is wrong. But if I spoke the truth, why did you strike me?" Then Annas sent him still bound, to Caiaphas the high priest.

And all the chief priests, elders and teachers of the law came together.

The chief priests and the whole Sanhedrin were looking for false evidence against Jesus so that they could put him to death. But they did not find any, though many false witnesses came forward.

Finally two came forward and declared, "We heard him say, 'I will destroy this man-made, temple of God and in three days will build another, not made by man.' "

Yet even then their testimony did not agree. At day break the high priest stood up and said to Jesus, "Are you not going to answer? What is this testimony that these men are bringing against you?" But Jesus remained silent.

The high priest said to him, "I charge you under oath by the living God: Tell us if you are the Christ, the Son of the Blessed One."

Jesus answered, "If I tell you, you will not believe me, and if I asked you, you would not answer.

"Yet, it is as you say," Jesus replied. "But I say to all of you: In the future you will see the Son of Man sitting at the right hand of the Mighty One and coming on the clouds of heaven."

Then the high priest tore his clothes and said, "He has spoken blasphemy! Why do we need any more witnesses? Look, now you heard the blasphemy. What do you think?"

They all condemned him as worthy of death.

The men who were guarding Jesus began mocking and beating him. They spit in his face and struck him with their fists others blindfolded him and demanded, "Prophesy! Who hit you?" And they said many other insulting things to him and the guards took him and beat him.

While Peter was below in the courtyard, one of the servant girls at the door of the high priest came by. When she saw Peter warming himself, she looked closely at him.

"You also were with Jesus of Galilee," she said.

But he denied it before them all. "I don't know what you're talking about," he said.

Then he went out to the gateway and the rooster crowed. Another girl saw him and said to the people there, "This fellow was with Jesus to Nazareth."

He denied it again, with an oath: "I don't know the man!"

About an hour later one of the high priest's servants, a relative of the man whose ear Peter had cut off, challenged him, "Didn't I see you with him in the olive grove?"

Those standing near said to Peter, "Surely you are one of them, for you are a Galilean. Your accent gives you away."

He began to call down curses on himself, and he swore to them, "I don't know this man you're talking about."

Immediately the rooster crowed the second time.[2] The lord turned and looked straight at Peter. Then Peter remembered the word Jesus had spoken to him: "Before the rooster crows twice you will disown me three times." And he went outside and wept bitterly.

(Mt. 27:3-10)

When Judas, who had betrayed him, saw that Jesus was condemned, he was seized with remorse and returned the thirty silver coins to the chief priests and the elders. "I have sinned," he said, "for I have betrayed innocent blood."

"What is that to us?" they replied. "That's your responsibility."

So Judas threw the money into the temple and left. Then he went away and hanged himself.

The chief priests picked up the coins and said, "It is against the law to put this into the treasury, since it is blood money." So they decided to use the money to buy the potter's field as a burial place for foreigners. That is why it has been called to Field of Blood to this day. Then what was spoken by Jeremiah the prophet was fulfilled: "They took the thirty silver coins, the price set on him by the people of Israel, and they used them to buy the potter's field, as the Lord commanded me."

(Mt. 27:1,2/Mk. 15:1/Jn. 18:28)

Very early in the morning, all the chief priests and the elders of the people came to the decision[3] to put Jesus to death. They bound him, led him away from Caiaphas to the palace of the Roman governor and handed him over to Pilate, the governor.

STUDY NOTES

1. While the Chief priests, elders and teachers of the law had come together in the house of the High Priest waiting for Jesus to be brought in, Jesus is taken to stand before Annas the father-in-law of the High priest. This indicates who was really in-charge.

2. It must have been early morning by now.

3. The conclusion reached earlier is endorsed here again. (*Final touches?!*)

XXX
THE ROMAN TRIAL

Day: 7 FRIDAY:
(Mt. 27:11-14/Mk. 15:2-5/Lk. 23:1-7/Jn. 18:28-38)

By now it was early morning, and to avoid ceremonial uncleanness the Jews did not enter the palace; they wanted to be able to eat the Passover. So Pilate came out to them and asked, "What charges are you bringing against this man?"

"If he were not a criminal," they replied, "we would not have handed him over to you."

Pilate said, "Take him yourselves and judge him by your own law."

"But we have no right to execute anyone," the Jews objected. This happened so that the words Jesus had spoken indicating the kind of death he was going to die would be fulfilled.

And they began to accuse him, saying, "We have found this man subverting our nation. He opposes payment of taxes to Caesar and claims to be Christ, a king."

The chief priests and the elders accused him of many things. Then Pilate asked him, "See how many things they are accusing you of. Don't you hear the testimony they are bringing against you?" Aren't you going to answer?"

But Jesus still made no reply, and Pilate was amazed.

Pilate then went back inside the palace, summoned Jesus and asked him, "Are you the king of the Jews?"

"Is that your own idea," Jesus asked, "or did others talk to you about me?"

"Am I a Jew?" Pilate replied. "It was your people and your chief priests who handed you over to me. What is it you have done?"

Jesus said, "My kingdom is not of this world. If it were, my servants would fight to prevent my arrest by the Jews. But now my kingdom is from another place."

"You are a king, then!" said Pilate.

Jesus answered, "You are right in saying I am a king. In fact, for this reason I was born, and for this I came into the world, to testify to the truth. Everyone on the side of truth listens to me."

"What is truth?" Pilate asked. With this he went out again to the Jews and said, "I find no basis for a charge against him.

But they insisted, "He stirs up the people all over Judea by his teaching. He started in Galilee and has come all the way here."

On hearing this, Pilate asked if the man was a Galilean. When he learned that Jesus was under Herod's jurisdiction, he sent him to Herod, who was also in Jerusalem at that time.

(Lk. 23:8-12)

When Herod saw Jesus, he was greatly pleased, because for a long time he had been wanting to see him. From what he had heard about him, he hoped to see him perform some miracle. He plied him with many questions, but Jesus gave him no answer. The chief priests and the teachers of the law were standing there, vehemently accusing him. Then Herod and his soldiers ridiculed and mocked him. Dressing him in an elegant robe, they sent him back to Pilate. That day Herod and Pilate became friends – before this they had been enemies.

(Mt. 27:15-31/Mk. 15:6-20/Lk. 23:13-25/Jn. 18:39-19:16)

Pilate called together the chief priests, the rulers and the people, and said to them, "You brought me this man as one who was inciting the people to rebellion. I have examined him in your presence and have found no basis for your charges against him. Neither has Herod, for he sent him back to us; as you can see, he has done nothing to deserve death. Therefore, I will punish him and then release him."

He said this because, now it was the custom at the Feast to release a prisoner whom the people requested.[1] At that time they had a notorious prisoner called Barabbas was in prison with the insurrectionists who had committed murder in the uprising. The crowd came up and asked Pilate to do for them what he usually did.

So when the crowd had gathered, Pilate asked them, "Which one do you want me to release to you - Barabbas, or Jesus who is called Christ?"

For he knew it was out of envy that they had handed Jesus over to him.

While Pilate was sitting on the judge's seat, his wife sent him this message: "Don't have anything to do with that innocent man, for I have suffered a great deal today in a dream because of him."

But the chief priests and the elders persuaded the crowd to ask for Barabbas and to have Jesus executed. Wanting to release Jesus, Pilate asked, "Which of the two do you want me to release to you?"

They shouted back, "No, not him! Give us Barabbas!"

"What shall I do, then, with Jesus who is called Christ?" Pilate asked.

They all answered, "Crucify him!"

"Why? What crime has he committed?" asked Pilate.

But they shouted all the louder, "Crucify him!"

Then Pilate took Jesus and had him flogged.

The governor's soldiers led Jesus away into the palace(that is, the Praetorium) and called together the whole company of soldiers.

They stripped him and put a scarlet robe on him, and then twisted together a crown of thorns and set it on his head. They put a staff in his right hand and knelt in front of him and mocked him. "Hail, king of the Jews!" they said. They spit on him, and took the staff and struck him on the head again and again.

Once more Pilate came out and said to the Jews, "Look, I am bringing him out to you to let you know that I find no basis for a charge against him."[2] When Jesus came out wearing the crown of thorns and the purple robe, Pilate said to them, "Here is the man!"

As soon as the chief priests and their officials saw him, they shouted, "Crucify! Crucify!"

But Pilate answered, "You take him and crucify him. As for me, I find no basis for a charge against him."

The Jews insisted, "We have a law, and according to that law he must die, because he claimed to be the Son of God."

When Pilate heard this, he was even more afraid, and he went back inside the palace. "Where do you come from?" he asked Jesus, but Jesus gave him no answer. "Do you refuse to speak to me?" Pilate said. "Don't you realize I have power either to free you or to crucify you?"

Jesus answered, "You would have no power over me if it were not given to you from above. Therefore the one who handed me over to you is guilty of a greater sin."

From, then on, Pilate tried to set Jesus free, but the Jews kept shouting, "If you let this man go, you are no friend of Caesar. Anyone who claims to be a king opposes Caesar."

When Pilate heard this, he brought Jesus out and sat down on the judge's seat at a place known as the Stone Pavement (which in Aramaic is Gabbatha). It was the day of Preparation of Passover Week, about the sixth hour.

"Here is your king," Pilate said to the Jews.

But they shouted, "Take him away! Take him away! Crucify him!"

"Shall I crucify your king?" Pilate asked.

"We have no king but Caesar," the chief priests answered.

For the third time he spoke to them: "Why? What crime has this man committed? I have found in him no grounds for the death penalty. Therefore I will have him punished and then release him."

But with loud shouts they insistently demanded that he be crucified, and their shouts prevailed.

When Pilate saw that he was getting nowhere, but that instead an uproar was starting, wanting satisfy the crowd, he took water and washed his hands in front of the crowd. "I am innocent of this man's blood," he said. "It is your responsibility!"

All the people answered, "Let his blood be on us and on our children!"

So Pilate decided to grant their demand. He released the man who had been thrown into prison for insurrection and murder, the one they asked for, and surrendered Jesus to their will.

STUDY NOTES

1. Jesus was not a condemned prisoner to be released thus. He was just a trial prisoner. Pilate fails to distinguish between the two and as a result of it, makes a Himalayan blunder in delivering justice.
2. Why flog Him if He was innocent?!

XXXI
THE SUFFERING AND DEATH

Day: 7 FRIDAY:
(Mt. 27:31-56/Mk. 15:20-41/Lk. 23:26-49/Jn. 19:16-37)
The Soldiers took charge of Jesus. They took off the robe and put his own clothes on him. Then they led him away to crucify him.

Carrying his own cross, he went out to the place of the Skull (which in Aramaic is called Golgotha). A certain man from Cyrene, Simon, the father of Alexander and Rufus, was passing by on his way in from the country, and they forced him to carry the cross.

A large number of people followed him, including women who mourned and wailed for him. Jesus turned and said to them, "Daughters of Jerusalem, do not weep for me; weep for yourselves and for your children. For the time will come when you will say, 'Blessed are the barren women, the wombs that never bore and the breasts that never nursed!' Then

" 'they will say to the mountains, "Fall on us!" and to the hills, "Cover us!" '

For if men do these things when the tree is green, what will happen when it is dry?"

Two other men, both criminals, were also led out with him to be executed.

They came to a place called Golgotha (Which means the place of the Skul). There they offered Jesus wine to drink, mixed with gall; but after tasting it, he refused to drink it.

There they crucified him, along with the criminals —one on his right, the other on his left. And the scripture was fulfilled which says, "He was counted with the lawless ones."

Jesus said, "Father, forgive them, for they do not know what they are doing."

It was the third hour when they crucified him.

Pilate had a notice prepared and fastened to the cross. It read: JESUS OF NAZARETH, THE KING OF THE JEWS. Many of the Jews read this sign, for the place where Jesus was crucified was near the city, and the sign was written in Aramaic, Latin and Greek. The chief priests of the Jews protested to Pilate, "Do not write 'The King of the Jews,' but that this man claimed to be king of the Jews."

Pilate answered, "What I have written, I have written."

When the soldiers crucified Jesus, they took his clothes, dividing them into four shares, one for each of them, with the undergarment remaining. This garment was seamless, woven in one piece from top to bottom.

"Let's not tear it," they said to one another. "Let's decide by lot who will get it."

This happened that the scripture might be fulfilled which said,

"They divided my garments among them

and cast lots for my clothing."

So this is what the soldiers did.

And sitting down, they kept watch over him there.

Near the cross of Jesus stood his mother, his mother's sister, Mary the wife of Clopas, and Mary Magdalene. When Jesus saw his mother there, and the disciple whom he loved standing nearby, he said to his mother, "Dear woman, here is you son," and to the disciple, "Here is your mother." From that time on, this disciple took her into his home.

The people stood watching. Those who passed by hurled insults at him, shaking their heads and saying, "You who are going to destroy the temple and build it in three days, save yourself! Come down from the cross, if you are the Son of God!"

In the same way the chief priests, the teachers of the law and the elders mocked him. "He saved others," they said, "but he can't save himself! He's the King of Israel! Let him come down now from the cross, and we will believe in him. He trusts in God. Let God rescue him now if he wants him, for he said, 'I am the Son of God.' Let him save himself if he is the Christ of God, the chosen one."

The soldiers also came up and mocked him. They offered him wine vinegar and said, "If you are the king of the Jews, save yourself."

One of the criminals who hung there hurled insults at him: "Aren't you the Christ? Save yourself and us!"

But the other criminal rebuked him. "Don't you fear God," he said, "since you are under the same sentence? We are punished justly, for we are getting what our deeds deserve. But his man has done nothing wrong."

Then he said, "Jesus, remember me when you come into your kingdom."

Jesus answered him, "I tell you the truth, today you will be with me in paradise."

It was now about the sixth hour [*Noon*], and darkness came over the whole land until the ninth hour, for the sun stopped shining.[1]

About ninth hour Jesus cried out in a loud voice, "Eloi, Eloi, lama sabachthani?" – which means, "My God, my God, why have you forsaken me?"

When some of those standing there heard this, they said, "He's calling Elijah."

Immediately one of them ran and got a sponge. He filled it with wine vinegar, put it on a stick, and offered it to Jesus to drink. The rest said, "Now leave him alone. Let's see if Elijah comes to save him."

Later, knowing that all was now completed, and so that the Scripture would be fulfilled, Jesus said, "I am thirsty." A jar of win vinegar was there, so they soaked a sponge in it, put the sponge on a stalk of the hyssop plant, and lifted it to Jesus' lips. When he had received the drink, Jesus said, "It is finished."

Jesus called out with a loud voice, "Father, into your hands I commit my spirit." When he had said this, he breathed his last.

At that moment the curtain of the temple was torn in two from top to bottom. The earth shook and the rocks split. The tombs broke open and the bodies of many holy people who had died were raised to life. They came out of the tombs, and after Jesus' resurrection they went into the holy city and appeared to many people.

When the centurion and those with him who were guarding Jesus saw the earthquake and all that had happened, they were terrified, and exclaimed, "Surely he was the Son of God!"

When all the people who had gathered to witness this sight saw what took place, they beat their breasts and went away.

[*As these were happening at Golgotha, there in the city....*]

Now it was the day of Preparation, and the next day was to be a special Sabbath. Because the Jews did not want the bodies left on the crosses during the Sabbath, they asked Pilate to have the legs broken and the bodies taken down. The soldiers therefore came and broke the legs of the first man who had been crucified with Jesus, and then those of the other. But when they came to Jesus and found that he was already dead, they did not break his legs. Instead, one of the soldiers pierced Jesus' side with a spear, bringing a sudden flow of blood and water. The man who saw it has given testimony, and his testimony is true. He knows that he tells the truth, and he testifies so that you also may believe. These things happened so that the scripture would be fulfilled: "Not one of his bones will be broken," and, as another scripture says, "They will look on the one they have pierced."

But all those who knew him, including the women who had followed him from Galilee, stood at a distance, watching these things.

Among them were Mary Magdalene, Mary the mother of James and Joses, and mother of Zebedee's sons and Salome.

(Mt. 27:57-61/Mk. 15:42-47/Lk. 23:50-56/Jn. 19:38-42)

Now there was a rich man named Joseph, a member of the Council, a good and upright man, who had not consented to their decision and action. He came from the Judean town of Arimathea and he was waiting for the kingdom of God.

Joseph was a disciple of Jesus, but secretly because he feared the Jews. It was Preparation Day (that is, the day before the Sabbath). So as evening approached, Joseph went boldly to Pilate and asked for Jesus' body. Pilate was surprised to hear that he was already dead. Summoning the centurion, he asked him if Jesus had already died. When he learned from the centurion that it was so, he gave the body to Joseph. So Joseph bought some linen cloth, took down the body, wrapped it in the clean linen cloth, and took the body away.

He was accompanied by Nicodemus, the man who earlier had visited Jesus at night. Nicodemus brought a mixture of myrrh and aloes, about seventy-five pounds. Taking Jesus' body, the two of them wrapped it, with the spices in strips of linen. This was in accordance with Jewish burial customs. At the place where Jesus was crucified, there was a garden, and in the garden a new tomb cut out of the rock by Joseph, in which no one had ever been laid. Because it was the Jewish day of Preparation and since the tomb was nearby, they laid Jesus there. He rolled a big stone in front of the entrance to the tomb.

And the Sabbath was about to begin Mary Magdalene and the other Mary were sitting there opposite the tomb. Saw the tomb and how the body was laid in it.

Then they went home and prepared spices and perfumes. But they rested on the Sabbath in obedience to the commandment.

STUDY NOTES

1. The three-hour darkness must have been a totally unexpected occurrence. The resultant confusion can well be imagined. Soldiers who were guarding Jesus and the thieves, standing there with lamps at mid-day!

XXXII

THE TOMB SEALED (SATURDAY THE SABBATH)

Day: 8 SATURDAY (SABBATH):

(Mt. 27:62-66)

The next day, the one after Preparation Day, the chief priests and the Pharisees went to Pilate. "Sir," they said, "we remember that while he was still alive that deceiver said, 'After three days I will rise again.' So give the order for the tomb to be made secure until the third day. Otherwise, his disciples may come and steal the body and tell the people that he has been raised from the dead. This last deception will be worse than the first.

"Take a guard," Pilate answered. "Go, make the tomb as secure as you know how." So they went and made the tomb secure by putting a seal on the stone and posting the guard.

HE HAS RISEN JUST AS HE SAID

XXXIII
THE FIRST DAY OF THE WEEK (SUNDAY)

Day: 9 SUNDAY:
(Mt. 28:1/Mk. 16:1,2/Lk. 24:1/Jn. 20:1)
¹After the Sabbath, at down on the first day of the week, while it was still dark, Mary Magdalene, Mary the mother of James, and Salome took the spices they had prepared and went to the tomb so that they might go to anoint Jesus' body.

(Mk. 16:3)
And they asked each other, "Who will roll the stone away from the entrance of the tomb?"
[*As the women approached the tomb, there in the site of the tomb......*]

(Mt. 28:2-4)
There was a violent earthquake, for an angel of the Lord came down from heaven and, going to the tomb, rolled back the stone and sat on it. His appearance was like lightning, and his clothes were white as snow. The guards were so afraid of him that they shook and became like dead men.

(Mk. 16:4,5/Lk. 24:2-4/Jn. 20:1,2)
[*The women reach the tomb*]
But when they looked up they saw that the stone which was very large had been rolled away from the tomb [*The guards have fled by now*], but when they entered, they did not find the body of the Lord Jesus. While they were wondering about this,

(So) she [*Mary Magdalene*]went running.[*to pass this bad news that body of Christ is missing*]

(Mt. 28:5-8/Mk. 16:5-8/Lk. 24:3-9)

[*After Mary Magdalene had left the tomb in an impulse to inform the disciples of this development, others stay there too stunned to react not knowing what to do.....*]

While they were wondering about this, suddenly two men in clothes that gleamed like lightning stood beside them. In their freight the women bowed down with their faces to the ground. "Don't be alarmed," he said, "I know that you are looking for Jesus the Nazarene who was crucified. Why do you look for the living among the dead? He is not here; he has risen, just as he said. Come and see the place where he lay. Remember how he told you, while he was still with you in Galilee.

"The Son of Man must be delivered into the hands of sinful men, be crucified and on the third day be raised again.

"Then go quickly and tell his disciples[2] and Peter 'he has risen from the dead and is going ahead of you into Galilee. There you will see, just as he told you.' Now I have told you." Then they remembered his words; so the women hurried away from the tomb afraid yet filled with joy. Trembling and bewildered the women went out and fled from the tomb. They said nothing to anyone, because they were afraid.

(Mk. 16:9,10/Jn. 20:2-17)

[*In the mean time Mary Magdalene*] came running to Simon and the other disciple, the one Jesus loved and said, "They have taken the Lord out of the tomb, and we don't know where they had put him!"

So Peter and the other disciple started for the tomb. Both were running, but the other disciple outran Peter and reached the tomb first. He bent over and looked in at the strips of linen, lying there but did not go in. Then Simon Peter, who was behind him, arrived and went into the tomb. He saw the strips of linen lying there, as well as the burial cloth that had been around Jesus' head. The cloth was folded up by itself, separate from the linen. Finally the other disciple, who had reached the tomb first, also went inside. He saw and believed [*what Mary had said*] (They still did not understand from Scripture that Jesus had to rise from the dead.)

Then the disciples went back to their homes, but Mary stood outside the tomb crying. As she wept, she bent over to look into the tomb and saw two angels in while, seated where Jesus' body had been, one at the head and the other at the foot.

They asked her, "Woman, why are you crying?"

"They have taken my Lord away," she said, "and I don't know where they have put him." At this, she turned around and saw Jesus standing there, but she did not realize that it was Jesus.

"Woman," he said, "why are you crying? Who is it you are looking for?"

Thinking he was the gardener, she said, "Sir, if you have carried him away, tell me where you have put him, and I will get him."

Jesus said to her, "Mary."

She turned toward him and cried out in Aramaic, "Rabboni!" (which means Teacher).

Jesus said, "Do not hold on to me, for I have not yet returned to the Father. Go instead to my brothers and tell them, 'I am returning to my Father and your Father, to my God and your God.' "

[*Thus*] When Jesus rose early on the first day of the week, he appeared first to Mary Magdalene, out of whom he had driven seven demons.

(Mt. 28:9-15)

[*Meanwhile, as the other women were on their way to convey the good news to the disciples......*]

Suddenly Jesus met them. "Greetings," he said. They came to him, clasped his feet and worshiped him. Then Jesus said to them, "Do not be afraid. Go and tell my brothers to go to Galilee; there they will see me."

While the women were on their way, some of the guards. [*Some? Where did the other guards go?*] went into the city and reported to the chief priests everything that had happened. When the chief priests had met with the elders and devised a plan, they gave the soldiers a large sum of money, telling them, "You are to say, 'His disciples came during the night and stole him away while we were asleep.' If this report gets to the governor, we will satisfy him and keep you out of trouble." So the soldiers took the money and did as they were instructed. And this story has been widely circulated among the Jews to this very day.

(Mk. 16:10,11/Lk. 24:9-11/Jn. 20:18)

They [*Mary Magdalene and the others together*] went and told all these things those who had been with him and who were mourning and weeping. It was Mary Magdalene, Joanna, Mary the mother of James, and the others with them who told this to the apostles. But they did not believe the women, because their words seemed to them like nonsense. [*More so because, Peter and John have just returned after verifying Mary Magdalene's earlier story and the empty tomb*].

(Lk. 24:12)

Peter, however, got up and ran to the tomb[3]. Bending over, he saw the strips of linen lying by themselves, and he went away, wondering to himself what had happened.

(Mk. 16:12,13/Lk. 24:13-35)

Now that same day two of them were going to a village called Emmaus, about seven miles from Jerusalem. They were talking with each other about everything that had happened As they talked and discussed these things with each other, Jesus himself came up and walked along with them; but they were kept from recognizing him.

He asked them, "What are you discussing together as you walk along?"

They stood still, their faces downcast. One of them, named Cleopas, asked him, "Are you only a visitor to Jerusalem and do not know the things that have happened there in these days?"

"What things?" he asked.

"About Jesus of Nazareth," they replied. "He was a prophet, powerful in word and deed before God and all the people. The chief priests and our rulers handed him over to be sentenced to death, and they crucified him; but we had hoped that he was the one who was going to redeem Israel. And what is more, it is the third day since all this took place. In addition, some of our women amazed us. They went to the tomb early this morning but didn't find his body. They came and told us that they had seen a vision of angels, who said he was alive. Then some of our companions went to the tomb and found it just as the women had said, but him they did not see."

He said to them, "How foolish you are, and how slow of heart to believe all that the prophets have spoken! Did not the Christ have to suffer these things and then enter his glory?" And beginning with Moses and all the Prophets, he explained to them what was said in all the Scriptures concerning himself.

As they approached the village to which they were going, Jesus acted as if he were going farther. But they urged him strongly, "Stay with us, for it is nearly evening; the day is almost over." So he went in to stay with them.

When he was at the table with them, he took bread, gave thanks, broke it and began to give it to them. Then their eyes were opened and they recognized him, and he disappeared from their sight. They asked each other, "Were not our hearts burning within us while he talked with us on the road and opened the Scriptures to us?"

They got up and returned at once to Jerusalem. There they found the Eleven and those with them, assembled together and saying, "It is true! The Lord has risen and has appeared to Simon." Then the two told what had happened on the way, and how Jesus was recognized by them when he broke the bread. But they did not believe them either.

(Mk. 16:14-18/Lk. 24:36-49/Jn. 20:19-25)

Later on the evening of that first day of the week, Jesus appeared to the Eleven as they were eating and while they were talking about this. With the doors locked for the fear of the Jews, Jesus came and stood among them and said, "Peace be with you they were startled and frightened, thinking they saw a ghost. He said to them, "Why are you troubled, and why do doubts arise in your minds? Look at my hands and my feet. It is myself! Touch me and see; a ghost does not have flesh and bones, as you see I have."

When he had said this, he showed them his hands and feet. He rebuked them for their lack of faith and their stubborn refusal to believe those who had seen him after he had risen.

And while they still did not believe it because of joy and amazement, he asked them, "Do you have anything here to eat?" They gave him a piece of broiled fish, and he took it and ate it in their presence.

He said to them, "This is what I told you while I was still with you: Everything must be fulfilled that is written about me in the Law of Moses, the Prophets and the Psalms."

Then he opened their minds so they could understand the Scriptures. He told them, "This is what is written: The Christ will suffer and rise from the dead on the third day, and repentance and forgiveness of sins will be preached in his name to all nations, beginning at Jerusalem. You are witnesses of these things. As the Father has sent me I am sending you.

"I am going to send you what my Father has promised, but stay in the city until you have been clothed with power from on high."

And with that, he breathed on them and said, "Receive the Holy Spirit. If you forgive anyone his sins, they are forgiven; if you do not forgive them, they are not forgiven."

He said to them, "Go into all the world and preach the good news to all creation. Whoever believes and is baptized will be saved, but whoever does not believe will condemn. And these signs will accompany those who believe: In my name, they will drive out demons; they will speak in new tongues; they will pick up snakes with their hands; and when they drink deadly poison, it will not hurt them at all; they will place their hands on sick people, and they will get well."

Now Thomas (called Didymus), one of the Twelve, was not with the disciples when Jesus came. So the other disciples told him, "We have seen the Lord!"

But he said to them, "Unless I see the nail marks in his hands and put my finger where the nails were, and put my hand into his side, I will not believe it."

(Jn. 20:26-29)

A week later his disciples were in the house again,[4] and Thomas were with them. Though the doors were locked, Jesus came and stood among them and said, "Peace be with you!" Then he said to Thomas, "Put your finger here; see my hands. Reach out your hand and put it into my side. Stop doubting and believe."

Thomas said to him, "My Lord and my God!"

Then Jesus told him, "Because you have seen me, you have believed; blessed are those who have not seen and yet have believed."

STUDY NOTES

1. A casual reading of the related gospel passages giving the resurrection of Christ is sure to confuse the reader- since many details appear to be contradictory. But when studied in depth the very same passages give a crystal clear description of the incident.

2. As Mary Magdalene had gone to convey the bad news that the body of Jesus has been stolen, others are asked to go and convey the good news that 'He has risen'.

3. Peter wants to check it anyway, so he goes for the second time – this time alone. Unlike his earlier visit, he prefers not to enter the tomb.
4. The disciples are still in Jerusalem instead of going to Galilee!

• 201 •

XXXIV
RESURRECTED JESUS - BACK IN GALILEE

(Jn. 21:1-24)

Afterward Jesus appeared again to his disciples, by the Sea of Tiberias.[1] It happened this way: Simon Peter, Thomas (called Didymus), Nathanael from Cana in Galilee, the sons of Zebedee, and two other disciples were together. "I'm going out to fish," Simon Peter told them, and they said, "We'll go with you." So they went out and got into the boat, but that night they caught nothing.

Early in the morning, Jesus stood on the shore, but the disciples did not realize that it was Jesus.

He called out to them, "Friends, haven't you any fish?"

"No," they answered.

He said, "Throw your net on the right side of the boat and you will find some." When they did, they were unable to haul the net in because of the large number of fish.

Then the disciple whom Jesus loved said to Peter, "It is the Lord!" As soon as Simon Peter heard him say, "It is the Lord," he wrapped his outer garment around him (for he had taken it off) and jumped into the water. The other disciples followed in the boat, towing the net full of fish, for they were not far from shore, about a hundred yards. When they landed, they saw a fire of burning coals there with fish on it, and some bread.

Jesus said to them, "Bring some of the fish you have just caught."

Simon Peter climbed aboard and dragged the net ashore. It was full of large fish, 153, but even with so many the net was not torn. Jesus said to them, "Come and have breakfast." None of the disciples dared ask him, "Who are you?" They knew it was the Lord. Jesus came, took the bread and gave it to them, and did the same with the fish. This was now the third time Jesus appeared to his disciples after he was raised from the dead.

When they had finished eating, Jesus said to Simon Peter, "Simon son of John, do you truly love me more than these?"

"Yes, Lord," he said, "you know that I love you."

Jesus said, "Feed my lambs."

Again Jesus said, "Simon son of John, do you truly love me?"

He answered, "Yes, Lord, you know that I love you."

Jesus said, "Take care of my sheep."

The third time he said to him, "Simon son of John, do you love me?"

Peter was hurt because Jesus asked him the third time, "Do you love me?" He said, "Lord, you know all things; you know that I love you."

Jesus said, "Feed my sheep. I tell you the truth, when you were younger you dressed yourself and went where you wanted; but when you are old you will stretch out your hands, and someone else will dress you and lead you where you do not want to go." Jesus said this to indicate the kind of death by which Peter would glorify God. Then he said to him, "Follow me!"

Peter turned and saw that the disciple whom Jesus loved was following them. (This was the one who had leaned back against Jesus at the supper and had said, "Lord, who is going to betray you?") When Peter saw him, he asked, "Lord, what about him?"

Jesus answered, "If I want him to remain alive until I return, what is that to you? You must follow me." Because of this, the rumor spread among the brothers that this disciple would not die. But Jesus did not say that he would not die; he only said, "If I want him to remain alive until I return, what is that to you?"

This is the disciple who testifies to these things and who wrote them down. We know that his testimony is true.

(Mt. 28:16-20)

Then the eleven disciples went to Galilee, to the mountain where Jesus had told them to go. When they saw him, they worshiped him; but some doubted. Then Jesus came to them and said, "All authority in heaven and on earth has been given to me. Therefore go and make disciples of all nations, baptizing them in the name of the Father and of the Son and of the Holy Spirit, and teaching them to obey everything I have commanded you. And surely I am with you always, to the very end of the age."

(Acts 1:3)

After his suffering, he showed himself to these men and gave many convincing proofs that he was alive. He appeared to them over a period of forty days and spoke about the kingdom of God.

STUDY NOTES

1. Jesus had ordered the disciples to go to a particular mountain in Galilee but here they are, in the Sea of Tiberias- fishing!

XXXV

TAKEN UP INTO HEAVEN - AT THE MOUNT OF OLIVES

(Mk. 16:19/Lk. 24:50-53/Acts 1:4-14)

On one occasion [*in Jerusalem for the last time*], while he was eating with them, he gave them this command: "Do not leave Jerusalem, but wait for the gift my Father promised, which you have heard me speak about. For John baptized with water, but in a few days you will be baptized with the Holy Spirit."

So when they met together, they asked him, "Lord, are you at this time going to restore the kingdom to Israel?"

He said to them: "It is not for you to know the times or dates the Father has set by his own authority. But you will receive power when the Holy Spirit comes on you; and you will be my witnesses in Jerusalem, and in all Judea and Samaria, and to the ends of the earth."

When he had led them to the vicinity of Bethany, after he said this, he lifted up his hands and blessed them. While he was blessing them he left them and was taken up into heaven before their very eyes and a cloud hid him from their sight. Thus after the Lord Jesus had spoken to them, he was taken up into heaven and he sat at the right hand of God.

They were looking intently up into the sky as he was going, when suddenly two men dressed in white stood beside them. "Men of Galilee," they said, "why do you stand here looking into the sky? This same Jesus, who has been taken from you into heaven, will come back in the same way you have seen him go into heaven."

Then they worshiped him and returned to Jerusalem, with great joy, from the hill called the Mount of Olives, a Sabbath day's walk from the city. When they arrived, they went upstairs to the room where they were staying. Those present were Peter, John, James and Andrew; Philip and

Thomas, Bartholomew and Matthew; James son of Alphaeus and Simon the Zealot, and Judas son of James. They all joined together constantly in prayer, along with the women and Mary the mother of Jesus, and with his brothers.

And they stayed continually at the temple, praising God.

(Jn. 20:30,31 / 21:25)

Jesus did many other miraculous signs in the presence of his disciples, which are not recorded in this book.

Jesus did many other things as well. If every one of them were written down, I suppose that even the whole world would not have room for the books that would be written.

But these are written that you may believe that Jesus is the Christ, the Son of God, and that by believing you may have life in his name.

XXXVI
THE INSTITUTION OF THE CHURCH

(Mk. 16:20/Acts 1:15-2:47)

In those days Peter stood up among the believers (a group numbering about a hundred and twenty) and said, "Brothers, the Scripture had to be fulfilled which the Holy Spirit spoke long ago through the mouth of David concerning Judas, who served as guide for those who arrested Jesus – he was one of our number and shared in this ministry."

(With the reward he got for his wickedness, Judas brought a field; there he fell headlong, his body burst open and all his intestines spilled out. Everyone in Jerusalem heard about this, so they called that field in their language Akeldama, that is, Field of Blood.)

"For," said Peter, "it is written in the book of Psalms,

"'May his place to deserted;

let there be no one to dwell in it,'

and,

"'May another take his place of leadership.'

"Therefore it is necessary to choose one of the men who have been with us the whole time the Lord Jesus went in and out among us, beginning from John's baptism to the time when Jesus was taken up from us. For one of these must become a witness with us of his resurrection."

So they proposed two men: Joseph called Barsabbas (also known as Justus) and Matthias. Then they prayed, "Lord, you know everyone's heart. Show us which of these two you have chosen to take over this apostolic ministry, which Judas left to go where he belongs." Then they cast lots, and the lot fell to Mattias; so he was added to the eleven apostles.

When the day of Pentecost came, they were all together in one place. Suddenly a sound like the blowing of a violent wind came from heaven and filled the whole house where they were sitting. They saw what seemed to be tongues of fire that separated and came to rest on each of them. All of them were filled with the Holy Spirit and began to speak in other tongues as the Spirit enabled them.

Now there were staying in Jerusalem God-fearing Jews from every nation under heaven. When they heard this sound, a crowd came together in bewilderment, because each one heard them speaking in his own language. Utterly amazed, they asked: "Are not all these men who are speaking Galilees? Then how is it that each of us hears them in his own native language? Parthians, Medes and Elamites; residents of Mesopotamia, Judea and Cappadocia, Pontus and Asia, Phrygia and Pamphylia, Egypt and the parts of Libya near Cyrene; visitors from Rome (both Jews and coverts to Judaism); Cretans and Arabs – we hear them declaring the wonders of God in our own tongues!" Amazed and perplexed they asked one another, "what does this mean?"

Some, however, made fun of them and said, "They have had too much wine."

The Peter stood up with the Eleven, raised his voice and addressed the crowd; "Fellow Jews and all of you who live in Jerusalem, let me explain this to you; listen carefully to what I say. These men are not drunk, as you suppose. It's only nine in the morning! No, this is what was spoken by the prophet Joel:

"In the last days, God says,
I will pour out my Spirit on all people.
Your sons and daughters will prophesy,
Your young men will see visions,
Your old men will dream dreams.
Even on my servants, both men and women,
I will pour out my Spirit in those days,
And they will prophesy.
I will show wonders in the heaven above
and signs on the earth below,
blood and fire and billows of smoke.
The sun will be turned to darkness
and the moon to blood
before the coming of the great and glorious
day of the Lord.
And everyone who calls

on the name of the Lord will be saved."

"Men of Israel, listen to this: Jesus of Nazareth was a man accredited by God to you by miracles, wonder and signs, which God did among you through him, as you yourselves know. This man was handed over to you by God's set purpose and foreknowledge; and you, with the help of wicked men, put him to death by nailing him to the cross. But God raised him from the dead, freeing him from the agony of death, because it was impossible for death to keep its hold on him. David said about him:

"'I saw the Lord always before me.

Because he is at my right hand,

I will not be shaken.

Therefore my heart is glad and my tongue rejoices;

my body also will live in hope,

because you will not abandon me to the grave,

nor will you let your Holy One see decay.

You have made known to me the paths of life;

you will fill me with joy in your presence.'

"Brothers, I can tell you confidently that the patriarch David died and was buried, and his tomb is here to this day. But he was a prophet and knew that God had promised him on oath that he would place one of his descendants on his throne. Seeing what was ahead, he spoke of the resurrection of the Christ, that he was not abandoned to the grave, nor did his body see decay. God has raised this Jesus to life, and we are all witnesses of the fact. Exalted to the right hand of God, he has received from the Father the promised Holy Spirit and has poured out what you now see and hear. For David did not ascend to heaven, and yet he said,

" 'The Lord said to my Lord:

"sit at my right hand

until I make your enemies

a footstool for your feet." '

"Therefore let all Israel be assured of this: God has made this Jesus, whom you crucified, both Lord and Christ."

When the people heard this, they were cut to the heart and said to Peter and the other apostles, "Brothers what shall we do?"

Peter replied, "Repent and be baptized, every one of you, in the name of Jesus Christ for the forgiveness of your sins. And will receive the gift of the Holy Spirit. The promise is for you and your children and for all who are far off- for all whom the Lord our God will call."

With many other words he warned them; and he pleaded with them, "Save yourselves from this corrupt generation." Those who accepted his message were baptized, and about three thousand were added to their number that day.

They devoted themselves to the apostles' teaching and to the fellowship, to the breaking of bread and to prayer. Everyone was filled with awe, and many wonders and miraculous signs were done by the apostles. All the believers were together and had everything in common. Selling their possessions and goods, they gave to anyone as he had needed. Every day they continued to meet together in the temple courts. They broke bread in their homes and ate together with glad and sincere hearts, praising God and enjoying the favor of all the people. And the Lord added to their number daily those who were being saved.

Then the disciples went out and preached everywhere, and the Lord worked with them and confirmed his word by the signs that accompanied it.

www.ingramcontent.com/pod-product-compliance
Lightning Source LLC
Chambersburg PA
CBHW031150160726
47991CB00015B/1811